PLACE OF PASSAGE

PLACE OF PASSAGE

Contemporary Catholic Poetry

Edited by David Craig and Janet McCann

Story Line Press
2000

Published by Story Line Press, Three Oaks Farm, PO Box 1240, Ashland, OR 97520-0055

This publication was made possible thanks in part to the generous support of the Nicholas Roerich Museum, the Andrew W. Mellon Foundation, and our individual contributors.

Book design by Lysa McDowell
Composition by Wellstone Publications

Library of Congress Cataloging-in-Publication Data

Place of passage : contemporary Catholic poetry / edited by David Craig and Janet McCann.
    p. cm.
  ISBN 1-885266-86-3 (alk.paper)
    1. Poetry--Catholic authors. 2. Poetry--Translations into English. I. Craig, David,
1951- II. McCann, Janet.

PN6109.3 .P59 2000
808.81'938282--dc21

00-027109

ACKNOWLEDGMENTS

We would like to thank all the poets and publishers, who have waived fees and royalties; all profits that would ordinarily go to editors, poets, and publishers will be donated to the Bishops' Relief Fund for the alleviation of hunger and suffering.

We would also like to thank Texas A&M student Kelly Zayas, whose excellent proofreading skills, biographical research, and writing abilities were of great use to us.

* * *

Carolyn Alessio's poem is printed by permission of the author. **Jan Lee Ande's** poems "The Franciscan," "On Fire," and "Elegy in the Graveyard" are printed by permission of their author. **Sarah Appleton's** poem "If these buds" was first published in *Studia Mystica*. "Occasionally the Print of Their Voices: A Nativity Poem" is from *Ladder of the World's Joy* (Doubleday, 1977). The poems are printed by permission of the poet. **William Baer's** poems "Magnum XL-200" and "Runway" are printed by permission of the author. **Kay Barnes'** poem "Leonie, the Problem Child, Explains" is printed by permission of the author. **Fr. Murray Bodo's** poems "Sonnet for Five Franciscan Sisters" and "On Hearing Gregorian Chant in the Abbey of Solesmes" are reprinted by permission of their author. "Sonnet for Five Franciscan Sisters" first appeared in *St. Anthony Messenger*. "On Hearing Gregorian Chant in the Abbey of Solesmes" first appeared in *Cistercian Studies Quarterly*. **Bruce Bond's** poem is printed by permission of the author. **Sean Brendan-Brown's** "Strolling from the Deli, Grocery-Laden" is printed by permission of its author. **Ernesto Cardenal's** "19th Century Traveler on the Rio San Juan," from *With Walker and Other Early Poems*, translation © 1984 by Jonathan Cohan, Wesley University Press, by permission of University Press of New England. **Mike Chasar's** "Religious Autobiography" is copyrighted by the Christian Century Foundation. It is reprinted by permission from *The Christian Century*. **William Bedford Clark's** "Adoration at 2 A.M." is printed by permission of its author. **Chet Corey's** "Design" is printed by permission of its author. **David Craig's** poems are printed by permission of the author. **Pablo Antonio Cuadra's** poem "Horses in the Lake," translated by Grace Schulman and Anna McCarty de Zavala, is reprinted from *Songs of Cifar and the Sweet Sea*, translated by Grace Schulman and Anna McCarty de Zavala. Copyright © 1979, Columbia University Press. Reprinted with the permission of the publisher. **Robert Murray Davis's** poem "At the Christian Museum, Esztergom" is printed by permission of its author. **Bruce Dawe's** poem "Love Game" is reprinted by permission of *Southerly* and of the author. **Mark Decarteret's** poems "Sebastian, the Saint" and "Clare, the Saint" are printed by permission of the author. **Annie Dillard's** poems "My Camel, a Dialogue of Self and Soul," "God," "Christmas," and "Feast Days: Thanksgiving—Christmas" are reprinted from *Tickets for a Prayer Wheel* by Annie Dillard, by permission of the University of Missouri Press. Copyright © 1974 by Annie Dillard. **Fr. Jeremy**

TABLE OF CONTENTS

INTRODUCTION

THE POEMS OF THE HOLY FATHER

KAROL WOJTYLA

THE CHURCH YEAR IN POEMS

CHRIST THE KING

CHRISTMAS

EPIPHANY

ORDINARY TIME

✳ MERCY SUNDAY

✳ ASCENSION OF OUR LORD

✳ ASSUMPTION

✳ ORDINARY TIME

PLACE OF PASSAGE:
CONTEMPORARY CATHOLIC POETRY

For Catholics poetry is a major element of daily life, whether we think of it that way or not. There are many things in our lives that are burnished by their use in church ritual and by their place in the history of the faith. The familiar gleam of these concrete elements of faith serves to guide us through the hazards and ambiguities of contemporary life. Sacramentalism is the basis for the Catholic understanding of the visible and invisible worlds. For every one of us from the "casual Catholic" to the most orthodox believer, sacramentalism gives access to the sacred and defines our association with it. From birth to death, the living symbolism of the sacraments issues forth in words, and gives a sense of the numinous to daily experience.

Music is the further vehicle of our expression. Rhythms of all kinds direct our hearts and the words of our belief: the familiar hymns, rising and falling accents of the prayers, other kinds of rhythms of repetition — days of the week, seasons of the year, repeated patterns read about and lived. Liturgy, question and answer, rise and fall of remembered accents. Our Fathers, Hail Marys. These things are primary poetry. And then in our secondary poetry, we meditate or analyze or sometimes interrogate the primary poem that is our faith.

It tends to be this emphasis on the sacraments that distinguishes Catholic poetry from other kinds of Christian poetry. The symbols themselves are alive, points of contact between the daily and the divine. They allow active participation in the spiritual life. Unlike some notions of grace, the sacraments can be sought after; we do not have to merely wait and pray for them. The sacraments renew and refresh the believer, and the echoes of these most meaningful acts enrich literature. Baptism, the

Eucharist, Matrimony, Penance, Confirmation, Holy Orders, Extreme
Unction—in the old language or the new—comfort and define.

And things with which the sacraments are performed and associated
with have their own power, font and chalice, holy water, priestly ges-
tures. The performative act dissolves into the particulars that make it
up.   Then there are the little blessed things we tend to keep on our
persons: sacramentals, rosary, medal, scapular. We may keep old prayer
cards, stamped with the names of departed loved ones. Besides remind-
ing us of our religion, these things provide an enhanced sense of life in
this world and of the continuity from one generation to the next.

Lately there has been a renewal of interest in Christian literary study,
which has produced valuable books and essays. But the scholarship of
sacramentalism needs further development. Has anyone done a study
of the rosary in literature, as it appears in Chaucer, Shakespeare, Keats?
When the fictional characters are "telling their beads," usually an atmo-
sphere of reverence, expectation, or peace is being communicated. Some-
times there is a contrast between the faith of the bead-teller and the
attitudes of others. Sometimes a sense of the timeless is evoked. These
things may be done in subtle combination, as in Keats' "The Eve of Saint
Agnes," where the motif of the ancient "beadsman" helps to frame the
action and serves as commentary on it.

Of course, not all our poetry focuses on things. Some poetry is simply
prayer. Some is a form of scholarship—an attempt to understand a saint's
life, a historical incident, or a Church teaching. Some is autobiography,
showing how a Catholic upbringing shaped a mature perspective. (Some,
of course, is direct sermonizing—but we have tried to steer clear of that
here, opting instead for poems that illuminate rather than instruct.) Some
of these poems are expressions of pure joy at the gift of faith. What the
poems tend to share is this sense of the sacramental—the belief that there
are holy people, places, acts, and things, and God may be approached
through them.

What it means to be a Catholic today is not easily defined, and we
would not be able to formulate a credo for the book beyond what it says.
It is less difficult to discuss Catholic poetry, looking over and generaliz-
ing from what Catholics tend to write. Besides being in touch with the
numinous through the sacraments, the poetry also defines the points of
intersection between temporal and eternal through a sense of place. These
holy places of pilgrimage —physical and intellectual —are part of our
shared journey. This poetry has the quality of the magical inherent in
the belief, but its language is that of our tradition. Its times, places, and
seasons are defined by the Church.

Thus, in the most noted Catholic and other Christian poets of the past there has been a fusion of rhythm, however that may be defined, and passion. The work of St. John of the Cross has this urgency. It is differently present, but still there, in something like Francis Thompson's "The Hound of Heaven." The true Christian poets—saints or ordinary folks, Catholics and Protestant— often suffer from the feeling that the language of their experience lies just beyond them. They look for a transparent language with which to fix their experience of divinity, and find they are stuck with the opacity of words. The words both express and belie; every incomplete truth has something false in it, and we are painfully aware of this falling short. In the old dichotomy the poems tend to be Gothic rather than Hellenic verbal structures. There are of course exceptions, particularly in the Age of Reason, but by and large the poems are touched with that sense of the imperfect that is our nature, and because they know they can never be perfect, they dare more. They reach.

Catholics in all kinds of faith relations have written these poems. Some have the otherworldly perspective of John Henry Newman: Particulars are not in the forefront; the world's truths are metaphoric. The world, in substance, is a lesson. Others find the surface of the world as revealing, not fading against, the face of God. The glitter comes from God's presence, as He is the light behind and through things. These poems depict a transforming, redemptive nature. In the vanguard of this group are the poems of John Paul II and Thomas Merton.

Some of the poems are about being Catholic. They describe what it is like to live and grow among Catholics, and they create a powerful Catholic regionalism that involves time as well as place. Some of us experienced the eras when Catholicism and Protestants were more separate, more hostile to each other—when Catholic life was more flamboyantly "different." One poet recalls sitting in church and reading the pamphlets kept in the rack at the back about intermarriage between Cathy Catholic and Peter Protestant—a sure road to perdition for them both. Many remember having their friends grilled as to religious practices, and being forbidden to "hang around" with children from other religions. These poems, Catholic-ethnic as they might be called, share some of the particulars of Catholic culture of the various eras represented by the poets.

The Catholic's search for social justice and the fight against poverty and misery also figure into the poetry. The Catholic mythology includes the lonely figure in the jungle and the group of militant nuns. There are contemporary martyrs and saints, as well as people quietly doing good; we memorialize and celebrate them. The Catholic's duty to alleviate

poverty and injustice may be a significant motive for his or her poetry—
as may the experience of personal involvement in the missionary goal.

Of course, the saints of history are a major presence in this book. The
saints beguile us, each in his or her time period, example and touch-
stone. Emphasis on the saints is a distinctive feature of Catholic poetry.
In a sense they are like human sacramentals. They are a body of people
spread out through history whose holiness affects others throughout time.
The saints remind us of the actuality and possibility of miracle. They tell
us that God may intervene directly in our lives, set aside the physical
laws, restore the incurably ill, to His glory and our relief.

We have always identified with the saints in their histories and in their
desires. How many now middle-aged women once wanted to follow St.
Teresa—indeed, to be St. Teresa? How many men once saw themselves
as St. Francis, walking through the woods exuding holiness and making
friends with the animals? We made ourselves look the way we thought
they must have looked, said their prayers, overflowing with good will.
When we did not turn out all that saintly, the phase did us good any-
way—it replaced other, worse excesses of youth. And if we finally em-
braced what we had then chosen to give up (spouse, sex, family), we did
so with a heightened sense of their value. We have chosen saints' names
and we have our favorite saint still; we may ask St. Joseph to help us sell
our houses—or we may not. We may ask St. Anthony to help us find
our car keys, or St. Thomas Aquinas to help us write introductions to
anthologies.

The overwhelming pain and catastrophe that has characterized some
saints' lives may be encouraging to us, and others may not understand
this, accusing us of some kind of Schadenfreude or sadism. But the
saints were triumphant, and serve as examples. Their stoic endurance of
mythic horrors helps us to get through lesser difficulties. We try to imag-
ine them, reinvent their times. We may even rewrite them as our ideal-
ized selves—this way, we can at last "be" St. Teresa.

These poems sometimes reflect that the world is a bitter place, and
that sometimes the Catholic feels oppressed and helpless, and even out
of touch with the Church. And the poet may find that Catholicism itself
provides temptations and trials. The Dark Night of the Soul is a stage of
development that has artistic as well as spiritual effects on the poet. A
few of the poems show the search for faith: to find it, to hold on to it, and
to nourish it.

These poems, arranged to follow the rhythm of the liturgical year, are
layered with the richness of the Catholic life. Saints' days, seasons...can

we celebrate your name-day, Lydie? Let's have ice-cream... Catholic nostalgia, existential pain, precipices. Dark nights. Hard-won dawns. Questionable practices: leave this prayer in the church for nine consecutive days, then publish it. Catholic myths: did the nuns really tell you not to wear patent leather shoes? Catchwords and warnings. "Custody of the eyes." But even so, the eyes, the poets' eyes, escape custody. They cannot be manacled. They look. They take, and they reflect.

Contemporary Catholic poetry has been overshadowed by the Catholic novel, the powerful voice of which has echoed through the twentieth century in the tones of Graham Greene, Walker Percy, Francois Mauriac, and so many others. These novels show in mythic form the challenge to faith and to right living posed by the contemporary world. But twentieth-century Catholic poetry has its own distinctive accents. It is hoped that Catholics will find herein a thousand points of recognition, and non-Catholics will discover that texture that brings a different way of life closer, makes it real.

NOTE: The editors, presses, and poets here represented have all elected to donate their royalties and permissions fees to The Bishops' Relief Fund, for the alleviation of suffering worldwide.

It is to be noted also that in this anthology, no one is presumed to be responsible for or to agree with the words, ideas, or theological positions of other contributors.

THE POEMS OF
THE HOLY FATHER

Pope John Paul II is a fine poet, whose works have been translated into many languages. These poems which he has graciously allowed us to use are translated by Jerzy Peterkiewicz.

These philosophical reflective poems provided some of the direction of the anthology—as well as its name.

FEAR WHICH IS AT THE BEGINNING

1

Oh, how you are bound, place of my passage,
with the place of my birth.
God's design rests on the faces of passersby,
its depth following the course of ordinary days.

Sliding into death I unveil the awaiting, my eyes
fixed on one place, one resurrection.
Yet I close the lid of my body, and the certainty
of its decay I entrust to the earth.
You rise above it slowly, and level Your design
with the surface of each day,
and with the shadows of passersby in afternoon streets,
in the streets of our town at dusk.
You God, you alone
can retrieve our bodies from the earth.

2

This is the last word of faith going
to meet the necessity of passing,
the word that answers the record
not contradictory to being (death is contradiction),
the word most held in suspicion, uttered
despite everyday deaths,
despite this planet's history, which became
our place of passage, the place of death,
generation after generation.

3

Allow the mystery to work in me,
teach me to act within my body
suffused with weakness like a herald prophesying death,
like a cock crowing —
Allow the mystery to work in me, teach me to act in my
          soul
which intercepts the body's fear

and fears for that body —
the soul still has its fear for maturity, for acts —
shadows the human spirit carries forever —
and of the depth in which it was submerged;
finally of the divine, that fear
which is not against hope.

HOPE REACHING BEYOND THE LIMIT

1

Hope rises in time
from all places subject to death —
hope is its counterweight.
The dying world unveils its life again
in hope.

Young men in short jackets, hair failing on their necks,
pass in the streets, their sharp steps
cut into the space of that great mystery which
in every one of them stretches
between his own death and his own hope;
space leaping upward like the splash of the sun:
the stone rolled back from the door of death.

2

In that space — the world's fullest dimension.
You are
and therefore both I
and my slow fall to the grave
have meaning:
my passage unto death;
the decay turning me to dust of unrepeatable atoms
is a particle of Your Pasch.

3

I wander on the narrow pavement of this earth,
traffic hurtles by,
rockets shoot to space —
in all this
there is a centrifugal flow
(man, a fragment of the world differently set in motion),
this movement does not touch the core of eternity,
it frees no one from death
(man, a fragment of the world differently set in motion),
so I wander on the narrow pavement of this earth,

not turning aside from Your Countenance
unrevealed to me by the world.

4

But death is the experience of the limit,
it has something of annihilation,
I use hope to detach my own self,
I must tear myself away
to stand above annihilation.
And then from all sides they call and will call out:
"You are mad, Paul, you are mad."*
I wrestle with myself,
with so many others I wrestle
for my hope.

No layer in my memory alone
confirms my hope,
no mirror of passage recreates my hope,
only Your paschal Passage,
welded to the deepest record of my being.

5

And so I am inscribed in You
by hope,
outside You I cannot exist—
if I place my own self above death
and tear it from the ground of destruction,
it is because the self is inscribed in You
as in the Body which fulfils its power
over each human body
so my own self can be built again;
taken from the ground of my death it has a different contour
yet so very true,
in which my soul's body and my body's soul are again
          together,
and my earthbound being rests finally on the Word,
forgetting all pain as does the heart struck by the sudden
          Wind—
which no man can bear.

And the forests' crowns are rent, and their roots below.
That wind stirred by Your hand now becomes Silence.

6

The atoms of primordial man bind the ancient soil of the world
which touch with my death
to transplant it, ultimately, into myself,
so that each atom can become your Pasch, or — the *Passage*.

*Festus said with a loud voice, 'Paul, you are mad; your great learning is turn-
ing you mad'" (Acts 26:24).

MYSTERIUM PASCHALE

1

You cannot stop the passing currents. They are many.
They mill around, form a field where
you yourself pass, reconciled
because after all something does surge;
the world grows round you.
Also in me
something of inheritance remains, something of promise;
the passing current is the current that surges,
and you can bear neither current to the end —
both will flow on — you will fall lower,
this you know for certain;
you turn to dust,
this you know for certain. You exist
always deathbound, bound always to the future
which always steps into your current.
But will it free you from the fields that pass?
will it seize all past from existence,
and all future too?

2

Mysterium paschale,
the mystery of Passage
in which the order of passing is reversed,

since we pass from life to death —
such is the experience, and the obviousness therein.

For passing through death toward life is mystery.
Mystery — a deep record
as yet unread to the very end,
apprehended, not contrary to being
(is death not more contrary?).

If that One unveils the record,
reads it, tests it on himself, and
Passes Over,

only then we touch the traces
and take the sacrament in which
He who went remains—
and so, still passing toward death,
we stay in that space called mystery.

3

You cannot stop the passing currents. They are many. The
world grows on, reaching toward each human death,
entering the orbit of thought, of unrepeatable atoms: (man
records his heart beats in creation's passing flux, man
dies—higher than the surging world—falls below "the
world" he carried in himself and around himself; in his exit
he is smaller, buried in the web of creation by the dust of
unrepeatable atoms, still passing on—
no longer He,
but the World
which grows on human cinders).

4

One of us, one of many
crossed all passing currents,
changed the direction of field where everyone passes,
solitary grandeur in all creation
unrepeatable.
This Passage is called *Pascha*—
mysterium:
First they ran to a grotto with animals as in a stable—
and from afar they followed the star;
then they ran to the grave—empty,
filled with luminosity,
then they climbed from the valley, steeply from Cedron's stream
under the city's overhanging cliffs
where they had put Him to death.
And all those links in His death
(the valley, the stream, the cliffs, the city)
he has divided—
and rolls back not only the tombstone
but the whole earth,
transforming the fields of passage,

though the stream of Cedron falls as before,
and as before, the stream of blood in man's body
steers toward death.
In each he planted a place of birth,
in each he unveiled a place of life
which grows beyond the passing current,
grows, beyond death.
This place in the midst of a surging world
resists death: it also receives the resurrection
as simplest ignorance, the fullness of faith
as ferment
which gives the lie to the surging world.

THE CHURCH YEAR IN POEMS

CHRIST THE KING

November 22: St. Cecelia

GRATEFUL

Be grateful that you live
Inside the head you do.
How many times have you
Gone sailing through
Your bed or favorite chair to
Wave a sign in the sleaze
Of traffic: Need money, *Please!*

How many times have you
Suffered with the losers
Of war, or chafed and simmered
On a reservation, or brokered
The rescue of many from fear?
How many hours have you
Survived the lessons of gender

Change, or held your hero,
So splendid because of you?
Be grateful. Be father and mother,
Be teacher, sister, and brother
In all that you dream and do,
Against the day your ledger
Is opened up to you.

PSALM # 1

He does not linger with scoffers
in the slow swirl,
bubbled stem of settled
bar beer, the loiterers'
golden climb.

He sweats all day in Presence,
mumbles among his tools.

How could he be moved?
He is the original natural man,
his laugh is the laugh of water.

Not so the wicked, not so.
He has no self
outside of God, sees what he is
as drives, no one behind the wheel;
chaff, before too many winds.

So how shall he stand–THEN?

The way of the wicked
is too wide for signposts.
It is a desolate field and offers
the nothing no one can take.

LABOR DAY THIS
HUNDRED YEARS

how is it possible
this national holiday would have
grover clevelands sanction
labor honored in the breach I guess
and we are here between summer and fall
an overcast and clammy day
and all of us waiting for the predicted
afternoon pregnant with sunshine
it is a little more difficult
celebrating this year you understand
what with the flags the parades
the town picnics and the raffles
peabody shutdown #10 in july
and three hundred miners
roofbolters and all went down as well
and in decatur the lockout goes on
the home grown company town benefactor
taken over and soured

I remember the night shift
wham of the cutter in the mill
how you waited on the frail light
before dawn and the noise of sparrows
or forking sixteen ounce cans into boxes
eight hours a day forty a week
or digging postholes in a six man crew
and I know what those
stalled bargaining sessions mean oh yes
so many open graves

have you been to el paso
have you seen the razor wire
looked across the rio grande to juarez
oh banditos in the canyons
oh banditos in the boardrooms
and who can drink the water

oh the days of the unions are over
sing the multinationals
dreaming of golden parachutes
have you been to the factories in haiti

this is the time for brothers
and for sisters in the soul
time for the blind man to open his eye
time when hunger is no longer a prayer
friends let us go on
let us take the good path
let us help one another
the orchards are filled with apples
we will slice them
and dip each slice in honey
and we will know how to
consecrate the day and the hour

12

san francisco in the museum
I have seen the eastern
eye of the archangel he will have
justice and strike this hours malice
backwards into the pit
if he can tell himself
today or tomorrow what is right
and what is not right
he is sitting there
gazing at something on the ground
which he perhaps does not see
this exhausted one
dressed in the linen
trappings of death
this veteran of the dirty wars

he does not care
about my space it makes
no difference to him
my crooked lines or narrow
or what I am thinking
about infinity

he says your ancestors
were no more mistaken
than you are

if you are hungry
you will find ashes
if you cut off your fingers
you will cry out

behind him
the larger elements
turn slowly
ominous in their power

I ask him
how shall I pray
he says
who are you

THEN SINGS MY SOUL

Who can tell a man's real pain
when h=-e learns the news at last
that he must die? Sure we all know
none of us is going anywhere

except in some pineslab box or its fine
expensive equal. But don't we put it off
another day, and then another and another,
as I suppose we must to cope? And so

with Lenny, Leonardo Rodriguez, a man
in the old world mold, a Spaniard
of great dignity and a fine humility,
telling us on this last retreat for men

that he had finally given up praying
because he didn't want to hear
what God might want to tell him now:
that he wanted Lenny soon in spite

of the hard facts that he had his kids,
his still beautiful wife, and an agèd
mother to support. I can tell you now
it hit us hard him telling us because

for me as for the others he'd been
the model, had been a leader, raised
in the old Faith of San Juan de la Cruz
and Santa Teresa de Avila, this toreador

waving the red flag at death itself,
horns lowered and hurling down on him.
This story has no ending because there is
still life and life means hope. But

on the third day, at the last Mass, we were
all sitting in one big circle like something

out of Dante—fifty laymen, a priest, a nun —
with Guido DiPietro playing his guitar

and singing an old hymn in that tenor voice
of his, and all of us joining in at the refrain,
Then sings my soul, my Savior God to thee,
How great thou art, how great thou art,

and there I was on Lenny's left, listening
to him sing, his voice cracked with resignation,
how great thou art, until angry glad tears
began rolling down my face, surprising me...

Lord, listen to the sound of my voice.
Grant Lenny health and long life. Or,
if not that, whatever strength and peace
he needs. His family likewise, and

his friends. Grant me too the courage
to face death when it shall notice me,
when I shall still not understand why
there is so much sorrow in the world.

Teach me to stare down those lowered horns
on the deadend street that shall have no alleys
and no open doors. And grant me the courage
then to still sing to thee, *how great thou art*.

November 22: St. Cecilia

A GUIDE TO MUSICAL STYLES I

There is a quality of supplication in the melody,
Ich ruf zu dir, I cry to thee,
as inside the plastic storage bin a tangled handful
of alfalfa hay breaks loose, and you lift out just enough—.

Their abrupt voices astound you; and the afternoon light's
three tonal calls in separate fugal entrance come:
we believe in one God, Wir glauben all
in einen Gott, to which refrain they throw themselves

against the shed in triumph, in delight
like some emphatic countersubject: light, dark, light.
This year the rains were not enough,
but when it's dry the mildew's down and the sheep are glad,

as in the simple sad chorales, O Haupt voll Blut und Wunden,
O sacred head once wounded.
They hear our footsteps scrape the gravel path.
Then out of the dusk suddenly you cling to me

and fill my mouth with wild sweet breath.
The smell of cedar, a cadenced high refrain appearing
repeatedly in the pedals, like the pealing
of bright bells the cricket code stops dead.

Swirling wind off the sea, toward a farm so close to shore,
the sea and scalloped face of the moon go down
stumbling through sills of trees
like a fanfare the final pedal part salutes.

A GUIDE TO MUSICAL STYLES II

The tragic feeling of the crucifixus is dispelled
by the jubilant chorus, the declaration,
and then the credo's swelling resurrexit, Lamb of God
have mercy on us. You remember

sudden rain was falling
with an animal's dark zeal, flowering oaks afflicted
but exultant, then the crashing of the downpour,
the little shed's metal roof, the small animals' cries inside.

Rivulets turned to flood, and every leaf and blade
was battered into motion.
Over the bass, upper voices in rapid figures rose.
You were racing toward the paddock to secure the gate,

stunned how the darkness had replaced
transparent light in which you'd almost felt conviction
that the adult heart bears this mercy,
can bear the sight of horses slowly parting

clumps of pasture with their hooves all day,
sounding the low white stones whose kingdom
shall never have an end, and the glory of the dusk.
The wild turkeys with their crashing wings

clamored toward the bordering trees,
where great limbs snapped and roared,
where the wind inhaled the lightning's flare,
a muttering, then the deeper register

with its implication of dejection, turned
by the hills to grief, rebounded,
then left a torpid growling.
You can never recover from such bounty,

wish only that you'd felt more terror
in every cell, the first scourging of more passion.
But already the rain's lightened into steady
aimless vigor, and your lamps restore the room.

A GUIDE TO MUSICAL STYLES III:
YET THE HARD CHAIN IS ON THE HEART

The scent of coffee flowers and mud blowing without need
to pardon, earth loosening and turning dusk into a compline hum,
shifting its weight as it darkens, stuck with leaves, a rustling of water
on the pond's serrate ledge, and the nearly invisible insects like
      wheat dust

thrown into the wind. The first motive, X, comprises a simple three-
      note
pattern, the pappus of groundsel, an octave between the goat shed's
      roof
and the chordal accompaniment of muted copper bells. Then Y,
impassioned as stems of yellow burgrass. So that we have to love
      necessity,

she says, giving the garden a final raking in the half-light, reluctant
to put away the tools, these clothes, her sweet-heavy hat edged in rain,
and matted gloves. Each seed its slit of earth, necessity clings to being
like E to E, vigorous and brilliant with no accidentals and no diver-
      sions.

And so dismounted in thigh-deep panicum, I'm bound in ceremony,
      and manacled
with racemes to the land, and stunned by the smell of our own dark
      clay
and the delirious rising Hear Ye Israel of wind and work.
      The skittish cattle
are going home, the sky is carnadine, then amber, then the sea's plagal
      cadence.

SYMPHONIA

Hildegard of Bingen at 80 before the prelates of
Mainz, 1178

Like a quill impelled to write
I saw myself in that same vision
God imprinted on my soul at birth.
Do not presume I come to confess
sins I have not committed.
The corpse was brought by priests
and all Bingen in procession.
A black cloud hovers to hurl a storm
of cries were the man exhumed.

Bittersweet hunger for sacred bread
gnaws at those who rightly buried
the man that you call rebel.
At Rupertsberg all ritual and song
have ceased, yet your proviso stings
most vilely. Hope of holy burial is balm
while we are living, incentive
for penance and right action. Loss
of final anointing chafes me sorely.

Too, the body cloaks a soul which speaks
its life through voice. What river of night
shuts the mouths of God's created?
Curve of shell and leaf resonate
as music and God's Word. His Son
takes flesh again each time we sing,
chanting melodies nine choirs
of angels hum and restoring symphonia
destroyed by Adam. Fingerlike
notes reflect celestial harmony
while such divine sounds of psaltery
and voice echo in our souls
to teach us love and thus rejoicing.

Proceed with care, most holy prelates.
This interplay of cymbals God intends.
Would you give Satan a trumpet,
play the discord he adores, and halt
the leap of souls to heaven?
Right you are to shuffle
and flip parchment. Remain
unmoved at your own peril.
Those who hold the keys of heaven
must be extremely careful lest
they close what should be open.

ADVENT

December 12: Our Lady of Guadalupe

THREE PRAYERS

Master of energy and silence
        Embracer of contradictions
Who withdraws behind death
        Like horizons we never touch
Who can be One and Many
        Like light refracting through glass,

Stepping in and out of logic
        Like a child unsure of the sea
In and out of time
        Like an old man dozing, waking,
In and out of history
        Like a needle through cloth,

Who we chase and bother with theories
        Who hides in equations and wind
Who is constant as the speed of light
        Who stretches over the Empty Place
Who hangs the Earth upon Nothing
        Who strikes like lightning.

~

Master of Light, my God,
Before whom stars tremble
And fall into themselves,

Who glows within each thing
Beyond reach of language
And deeper than silence,

Who passes through the Dark
That draws us towards death
And makes it one with you,

Whose Light is everywhere
Wherein I stand and see
My shadow disappear.

~

You do not speak to me of death.
You do not pester me, like some.

Far too busy with the universe,
Sometimes not busy enough,

Searching out our softer parts,
Trying to squeeze yourself in:

Showing off your famous night sky
Like a child with a new drawing,

Forever posing impossible problems
We try to solve like crosswords:

So when I wake and see the ceiling
Mottled like an old man's skin

I think of you,
When I imagine the grinning dead

I think of you,
And also when, at night,

I sometimes wake to find
A hand slowly stroking my thigh.

PRAYER FOR THE HARVEST

Tomorrow may we be all light,
Blessed with second sight
That brings the world to us
As children understand it.
The sweet mare in her stall
Will be still enough for all
Of us who whisper our confessions.
Come evening may we sleep all night
In the crooked arm of Mother Time
Where the owl's vigil calms us,
Where the fox in the harrowed field thrills us.
Tomorrow may we all be right
In every thing we say and do,
Forgiving ourselves our dispositions,
And those who can't forgive us.

ELEGY IN THE GRAVEYARD

Who will listen when we cry out
in the night? Inlets clot with
grief, the tunnels bend and crumple
with unknowing. Perhaps only one person
will rise to the challenge, and then
halfheartedly and tinged in green.

Look back down the line of becoming.
Odd beings whir and flitter in their
dazed and happy hopefulness.
Who are we to disappoint them—when they
put forth such effort as their small
hearts and fractured eyes allow.

The praying mantis on a limb genuflects
to the wind. Black-tailed prairie dogs
rise upright around their burrows,
awaiting the coming guest. Blackbirds
meditate in cedar trees, bodies blessed
in a flurry of flungdown light.

Beings seen and unseen make their
professions of faith. We, hapless
creatures, lie alone in our beds—
too distracted to find our knees,
too hoarse to utter prayers. Perhaps
some passing angel will remind us,
whisper the first words of supplication
in our behalf.

MEETING

You
You made me wait
You and I and this blank page
We are listening to my birthday rain
We are watching all the trees
Burst into October light.
How can we be waiting together
When I am waiting for you?
How can your impossible silence
Touch my face like a kiss?
How can my body end so precisely
At boot-soles, folds of clothes,
Curves of skin, ends of hair,
At the limit of my sight
On the misted, golden ridge
Where I am still looking for you,
When all of me is running out
Like photons spilling from a nova
And I am filling all that isn't you
With me
With my waiting,
So that when you touch
The least somewhere of time
You must touch me
Who am now the full horizon of emptiness?

And how could I
Be facing you there—
Dark to dark, nothing—
In the farthest shallows of everywhere
As all of tidy space
Sends its last bits foaming past me
Still so visibly, tangibly far
From your unmoving feet
Into the reaches of nowhere?
How could I when
Back here in October

You are waiting,
You and this now marked page,
With all the words I've ever written
And all the ones you've never said
Like bright forests of birthday leaves
For us to stroll in
Together?
We are watching all the world
Bloom into final light
And I wonder, Jesus,
Does it matter how or where at last
I touch you with my eyes
When I could be anywhere at all
With so confidently waiting
You here?

THE TIDE

Where is the Giver to whom my gratitude
rose? In this emptiness
there seems no Presence.

                    ❄

            How confidently the desires
            of God are spoken of!
            Perhaps God wants
            something quite different.
            Or nothing, nothing at all.

                    ❄

Blue smoke from small
peaceable hearths ascending
without resistance in luminous
evening air.
Or eager mornings — waking
as if to a song's call.
Easily I can conjure
myriad images
of faith.
Remote. They pass
as I turn a page.

                    ❄

            Outlying houses, and the train's rhythm
            slows, there's a signal box.
            People are taking their luggage
            down from the racks.
            Then you wake and discover
            you have not left
            to begin the journey.

*

Faith's a tide, it seems, ebbs and flows responsive
to action and inaction.
Remain in stasis, blown sand
stings your face, anemones
shrivel in rock pools no wave renews.
Clean the littered beach, clear
the lines of a forming poem,
the waters flow inward.
Dull stones again fulfill
their glowing destinies, and emptiness
is a cup, and holds
the ocean.

December 12: Our Lady of Guadalupe

THE VISION
for Terry Blackhawk

This is the part of your life
you're not prepared for: a tropical beach, Diamond Head
in the distance as predictable as a cliché,
a postcard back home on your refrigerator in Detroit.
Your husband and son are out there
somewhere, splashing in the Pacific. The salt water
         buoying up
their bodies like holy levitation.

But you—afraid of water—an anomaly
in this place, this chain of islands
surrounded by nothing but. Your pale
skin on this tanned beach screams out
haole—Hawaiian for ghost,
walking dead, body without breath.

So nothing prepares you for this vision:
Our Lady of Guadaleupe on Waikiki.
A blue ocean away from where she
first appeared to that dirt-poor
Indian peasant on Techopital Hill,
you can't miss her shape of glorious color coming
         towards you:
deep teal,
bright vermilion, bronzed gold tattooed
on the chest of a huge Mexican from Baja.
Even his back is emblazoned with her back
and you're stunned by the accuracy
of detail; the little angel at her feet
holding a sliver of the crescent moon
as if she were a living, breathing icon.

No, a holy card like the one you
always wanted in fourth grade. And not
just any holy card of any common saint:
Agnes with her lamb, Jerome with his lion,

Lucy with her eyes on a plate,
Thomas with his doubt. But the Mother of God
in all her human manifestations.

Mirror of Justice,
Seat of Wisdom,
Vessel of Honor,
Mystical Rose,
Tower of David,
Tower of Ivory,
House of Gold,
Gate of Heaven,
Star of the Ocean.

This ocean, this beach at your feet
as if she were Botticelli's Venus
washed ashore with the sea foam,
washed ashore for your approval.
And you tell yourself this isn't a miracle,
only a tattoo; this isn't anything
extraordinary, only your life. But
the vision makes your atheist heart
want to believe in God — or, at least,
His Mother — as the icon walks away
and you're left alone on the crowded
beach. The husband and son waving
impatiently for you to just
come on, come on, dive in.

CAREER DAY IN LA ESPERANZA

Dogs sleep along the sewage ditch,
women cross dusty streets
toting plastic strainers for tortillas.
Inside the cinderblock classroom,
children gape at the gringo volunteer,
who asks them what they want to be
when they grow up.
One boy offers *albañil*, bricklayer,
another says *co-piloto*, co-truck driver.
like the armed guard who sits atop the Pepsi truck.
Bilingual secretary, a girl says,
but the volunteer presses,
in slow and careful Spanish,
What about doctor? And lawyer?
She adds the feminine 'a'.
The children squirm.
A girl asks if ladies can be lawyers,
a boy in faded blue pajamas says
he's seen them on TV.
Bien, says the volunteer,
what about jobs in this village?
The children pick scabs from flea bites,
finger sagging shirt collars.
The volunteer looks out the window.
She remembers she came to learn.
On the street a vendor with a crooked leg
sells mangoes ripened like autumn leaves.
Two men shovel mud into wheelbarrows.
Rising above the street,
the only white-washed building in town.
What about the church, the volunteer says,
turning to the children,
Who is the boss of the church?
The girl who wondered about lady lawyers
gives her a sly look,
but the boy in blue pajamas shouts his
answer: *La Virgen*, the Virgin.

CHRISTMAS

FEAST DAYS:
THANKSGIVING—CHRISTMAS

I

Three things are too wonderful for me;
        four I do not understand:
the way of an eagle in the sky,
            the way of a serpent on a rock,
the way of a ship on the high seas,
                and the way of a man with a maiden.

                                    —Proverbs

Today I saw a wood duck
in Tinker Creek.
In the fall flood, look
what the creek floats down:
once I glimpsed
round the edge of a bank
a troupe of actors
rained in from Kansas,
dressed for comedy.
The flood left a candelabrum
on the lawn.
With a ten-foot hook
we fished from the creek
a bunch of bananas, a zither,
a casket of antique coins.

Or,
in the creek I found a log,
a tree trunk rotted halfway open.
Lord, lover, listen:
        I remember kissing on the stair
        dancing in the kitchen—
I crumbled the wet wood away.
Inside the tree a row of cells bad grown,
sealed chambers, smooth, elongate.
I slit one open, found a book

hand-bound in yellow thread:
a child's book of wildflowers
sketched in ink
and washed with watercolors.
  Come take a walk, you said.
  And if I reached out
  my hand could feel your shoulders move,
  thin, under your shirt.
What newness, what surprises!
Once I dug a hole to plant a pine
and found a ruby growing on a stone.

One thing we've got plenty of
here on the continents
is soil. Out of the soil
the plants are taking substance, edges,
like a tomato moving on its stake,
ten pounds of tomatoes, and the ground
blowing them up like balloons.
We walk on the soil
here on the continents
among the plants, and eat.

Thanksgiving: the men
are watching the game.
I wash, and dry, and dream.
I dream of a firelit room,
a tipi of eighteen buffalo hides,
of skins on the floor
and smoke curling up
the bark of the trunk of the lightwood lodgepole pine.

The Mandans in North Dakota
along the Missouri, prayed,
Go, flying birds, to the southern horizon,
to the old woman who never dies.
Return at the end of winter.
Carry sunshine, carry water
on your broad backs.

And in your beaks,
and in your beaks,
bring her blessing like a berry
to the crops you symbolize —
"The wild goose to the maize,
the wild duck to the beans,
the wild swan to the gourds."

Thanksgiving, creation:
outside the great American forest
is heaving up leaves and wood from the ground.
Inside I stand at the window, god,
with your name wrapped round my throat like a scarf.

Today I've been naming
the plants of the southern forest:
arrowwood, witherod,
hobblebush, nannyberry,
and the loblolly, longleaf
and shortleaf pine.

Lean through the willow, look
upstream, and see what's floating down!
I see camels swimming
with long-lash, golden eyes.
I see trunks and telescopes floating,
a canopied barge with silk scarves flying,
a peacock on each post,
and three crowned kings inside.
Caspar, Melchior, Balthazar,
I suspect you're on to something.

You tell me your dream
and I'll tell you mine.

I dreamed I woke in a garden.
Everywhere trees were growing;
everywhere flowers were growing,
and otters played in the stream, and grew.
Fruit hung down.

An egg at my feet
cracked, opened up,
and you stepped out,
perfect, intricate lover.

II

Woman, why weepest thou?
Whom seekest thou?

—John

December, and all its dark rains.
The apples in the cellar
are black, and dying inside their skins.
They pray all night in their bins,
but nobody listens;
they will be neither food nor trees.
Outside in the city
the cop wants to dig out his earmuffs,
the orange ones,
and if it were snowing he might,
but it's only rain.

God send us the springtime lamb
minted and tied in thyme
and call us home, and bid us eat
and praise your name.

God am I smug when they talk about Belsen—
I've never killed anyone in my life!
I simply betray:

let the phone ring,
seal a typed letter,
say to the girl in the courtyard,
"I never saw him before in my life,"
call a cab, pull on gloves,
and leave. And leave you,
and leave you with the bill.

"Home," I say to the cabby,
"home, driver, to Tinker Creek.
It's in Virginia."
And he says, "Sorry, honey,
you can't get there from here."
"Then driver, please," I say,
"put me to bed."

Take a hot bath; take
a cold shower.
In your mouth stick
a silver spoon
so you don't crack.

Today you hurt your hand
on the fireplace.
Tonight a Chinook
rose up from the south.
And my mouth
stuck shut,
my belly shook,
my eyes blinked hot,
and I went to the window.

There, stalking the lawn,
white tipis, wraith-like, ranged.
A smell of blood burned up.
The moon bruised down.
Antlers hung in the trees.
A thousand tipi doors lashed back,
void, like riven graves.

And in the creek,
in Tinker Creek,
a sky-high blackened hull rose up,
a red-stacked ocean liner, sailing upstream.

They're on the roof,
naked, but I bear them.
I remember reading

in my room, just reading,
and shutting the book,
and looking up,

and missing you, missing you,
and reading the paper again.
There's no freedom in it
or in fear:
my heart's not mine.
Once I went to the door
and an old black woman was there,
in a clown suit
and a clown's peaked hat,
and she carried a brown cloth bag.
Once an ape trailed through the hall
in my nightgown.
Once I surprised in the bathroom
the last of the Inca kings,
tall Atahualpa,
in his hand-stitched bat-skin robe.

"Don't worry," I said.
"It's all right," I said,
and ducked.

Oh, I've been here and there
around the heart —
a few night spots, really,
the kind that call themselves "Rathskellers,"
dim-lit, always changing hands,
and frequented on Sundays.
By the regulars:
mother in mink on the bar,
father looking up the grate to the sidewalk,
babies battling on the floor,
some sort of red-eyed monk
with a black-eyed mynah bird,
a clown (that clown!) —
and you,
variously:

weeping at the piano,
eating fly-blown meat with a spoon,
swirling a beer, and saying,
"Marry me"; or
"I read your letter
(diary, palm)"; or
"You don't understand."
And then always,
"Good-bye"
(So long, Take care) —
remember?
And then I leave.
I'm always the one who leaves.

God send us the springtime lamb
minted and tied in thyme
and call us home, and bid us eat
and praise your name.

III

And the captain of the Lord's host
said unto Joshua, Loose thy shoe
from off thy foot; for the place
whereon thou standest is holy.
                    —Joshua

I love with my hand, not my heart.
When I draw your face,
my fingers trace your lips.
Crossing a page, my hand keeps
contours; I know that art
is edges.
I touch when I type.
With every finger's tip
I travel the weave of the given.
Hand me a pencil,
cut off my head,
and I will draw you heaven.

Thank you, Squanto,
for the tip.
I knew something smelled funny in Iowa:
all that haddock, under the corn.
Mound-builders,
basketmakers,
cliff-dwellers —
all are gone to the sandhills.
Remember Sand Creek!
Remember Wounded Knee!
Remember how to fish?
You may have my salmon rights
to Tinker Creek.
Just keep off the roof;
it's coming up Christmas.

Under the water the wood duck
feels with his foot in the creek.

By day I cook, and we eat.
At night your band curls over my head,
curls into my hair as you sleep.
Hands curl up
like leaves. My hand curls up
from the fire to the tipi top
and out.
My hand curls down
the wood duck's throat.
In the curl of my hand I hold corn.

I kick through a forest of hands
by Tinker Creek. The sassafras hands
wear mittens; the tulip tree hands
demand money; "Wait!" cry the fraying hands
of a frivolous silver maple,
"I love you!"
A cottonwood hand floats down the creek
on its back, like Ophelia.

And deep on the banks of the creek
some hands uncurl;
some hands unleaf, and damply become
rich water,
wild and bitter perfume,
and loam, where bluets will bloom.

So your hand, asleep in my hair,
takes root, and flowers there.

Let me mention
one or two things about Christmas.
Of course you've all heard
that the animals talk
at midnight:
a particular elk, for instance,
kneeling at night to drink,
leaning tall to pull leaves
with his soft lips,
says, alleluia.

That the soil and fresh-water lakes
also rejoice,
as do products
such as sweaters
(nor are plastics excluded
from grace),
is less well known.
Further:
the reason
for some silly-looking fishes,
for the bizarre mating
of certain adult insects,
or the sprouting, say,
in a snow tire
of a Rocky Mountain grass,
is that the universal
loves the particular,
that freedom loves to live

and live fleshed full,
intricate,
and in detail.

God empties himself
into the earth like a cloud.
God takes the substance, contours
of a man, and keeps them,
dying, rising, walking,
and still walking
wherever there is motion.

At night in the ocean
the sponges are secretly building;
by day in a pharmacy drawer
capsules stir in their jars.
Once, on the musselshell,
I regenerated an arm!
Shake hands. When I stand
the blood runs up.
On what bright wind
did god walk down?
Swaying under the snow,
reeling minutely,
revels the star-moss,
pleased.

And to all you children out there with Easter bunnies
I would like to say this:
If they are chocolate, eat them.
If they are living, tuck them in your shirt.
There's always unseasonable weather.
Hose down the hutches.
For a special treat
to brighten up their winter
offer the early shoots of the wild American orchid,
the lady's-tresses,
in either of three varieties:
the slender, the hooded, or the nodding.

OCCASIONALLY, THE PRINT OF THEIR VOICES: A NATIVITY POEM

"But I, too, lacked the right to live"
said the red fox, standing at the edge of the barrow
some yearning in him...not afraid, really
as she listens to him

                         "And I"
said the bird bleeding in the shreds
of his throat, "I was once more
than hunger. Once from the tree
I saw..."

               The horse said nothing
his heavy head deep in the grass
smell, bowed down by his teeth

It was the fish who sang

like a file flashing over the gold

They waited...breathless
their love like an echo. The
pressure of a wing

As they, I can't see there
except occasionally, the print
of their voices

so I run into the stable
and rest in the warmth of the ox
the sound of their chewing

CHRISTMAS COLORS

There are advantages to coming late.
We crowd the chancel stalls this Freiburg night,
The winter lamps enough for those who wait
To sit within a splendor of old light

Shed to gladden Christmastide, a blaze
Out from the formal darkness, clothed in chancel white.
But richest gleamed the orchestra, that human maze
Where clear as mystery, music hid from sight.

Bowing through God's praise in Bach's great motion
The cellist's thin, white hair fell out of time,
A sudden movement slipped between the bows: one,
Two, three, scarlet drops shone bright as crime

Blazed like living holly on the wood.
In a grace not even Bach composed
The old man played; his formal linen moved,
Sleighted, in the rests of music, from his clothes,

To raise the blood or smooth it deeper in
The deepening veneer, just as its making chose.

CHRISTMAS

Trees that have loved
in silence, kiss,
crashing; the Douglas firs lean
low to the brittle embrace
of a lodgepole pine.

In cities at night
tin canisters eat
their cookies; the bed,
asleep, tossing,
brushes its curtain of bead.

My wristwatch grows
obscurely, sun-
flower big. Across
America, cameras gaze,
astonished, into the glass.

This is the hour
God loosens and empties.
Rushing, consciousness comes
unbidden, gasping,
and memory, wisdom, grace.

Birds come running;
the curtains moan.
Dolls in the hospital
with brains of coral
jerk, breathe and are born.

EPIPHANY

January 19: St. Anthony of the Desert

January 20: St. Sebastian

January 28: St. Thomas Aquinas

POETRY AND RELIGION

Religions are poems. They concert
our daylight and dreaming mind, our
emotions, instinct, breath and native gesture

into the only whole thinking: poetry.
Nothing's said till it's dreamed out in words
and nothing's true that figures in words only.

A poem, compared with an arrayed religion,
may be like a soldier's one short marriage night
to die and live by. But that is a small religion.

Full religion is the large poem in loving repetition;
like any poem, it must be inexhaustible and complete
with turns where we ask Now why did the poet do that?

You can't pray a lie, said Huckleberry Finn;
you can't poe one either. It is the same mirror:
mobile, glancing, we call it poetry.

Fixed centrally, we call it a religion,
and God is the poetry caught in any religion,
caught, not imprisoned. Caught as in a mirror

that he attracted, being in the world as poetry
is in the poem, a law against its closure.
There'll always be religion around while there is poetry

or a lack of it. Both are given, and intermittent,
as the action of those birds—created pigeon, rosella parrot—
who fly with wings shut, then beating, and again shut.

THE OPPORTUNITY

My father once, after his death,
appeared to me as a rose,
passed beyond intellect.
This time, he resumes
human form to become
a boy of six.
I kneel to hug him,
kiss the child's bare shoulder;
near us the ocean
sighs and murmurs,
firm sand reflects
the turn of the wave.

This is my chance to tell him,
"Much has happened, over the years,
many travels.
In the world,
in myself.
Along the way,
I have come to believe
the truth of what you believe."

The child, with good grace,
permits
my brief embrace, he smiles:
the words
are lazy waves above and around him,
he absorbs their tone,
knows he is loved.
Knows only that.

This was my chance
to speak, I've taken it,
we are both content.

CREATURES WHO MUST KNOW
BETTER HAVE TAKEN ME FOR
A BLOSSOM

This year Kennebec and Red Pontiac,
last year's russet and white kobblers
done in by nematodes, flea beetles,
early and late blight. Maybe it's
the 1/4 Irish blood that's made me drunk
with promise, though wasn't it Ali,
stung by his loss to Holmes,
who explained it, "I had the world,
and let me tell you, it wasn't nothing"?
You see, I cut them as if they were diamonds,
with a studied, precise stroke. *All this*,
the voice reason reminds me,
for what could buy in a reusable
mesh bag. But I'm stubborn
in the middle of God's own metaphor
dropping potatoes into loamy dirt,
while ruby-throated hummingbirds
take my red shirt for the biggest bee balm
they've ever seen. Their wings flapping
at an angel's pace, they taste my only
holiness, my sweat. I want to tell
my father what's happened, tell him
I'm sorry, I didn't mean to drink too much
and sleep it off on the job he got me,
didn't mean to get caught by a man named Earl
who has no eyebrows and was his boss.
None of that was planned any more
than he'd planned on the family's
Salvation Army clothes, his cars that never ran,
those late night trips upstairs to bleed
the radiators, or turn off a fan,
any reason to stand a while
and watch us sleep. After Mass

the children would go to grandmother's garden
to weed, water, and sometimes dig dinner
in our underwear, while she washed
our Sunday suits and we kids pretended
to be flowers.

RED FOXES

Insomnia pushed Nessa over the falls,
Her boat made of nothing but her own skin.
Deep in the comforter she curled like a baby
Waiting for sleep to return. Under the down
She willed herself a dream, but nothing came.
Nothing but cold and the prickly, pre-dawn stillness.
As fast as a ghost she stepped out of her sleeper,
Pulled on her woolen shirt and knee-high socks,
Her jeans and Red Wing boots. The glowing clock
Read three as Nessa hustled to the window
Above the field of young rye grass. The crop
Lay under the fog like a military haircut
Waiting to explode in warmer weather,
But winter always stayed too long. She tiptoed
Past her parents' room and down the stairs.
Nessa wondered how they could sleep tonight.

Bundled up in a coat, a hat and gloves,
She headed for the field beyond the barn
And longed for the voice to call her —
                              "Come into the field
Where all of us are living out our time."

Instead, not very high up in the fog
She heard the staggered honks of migrating geese.
They reminded her of students on a bus
Who squirm and *yak yak yak* to steer the time.
And *did* the leader really know the way?
She shivered, thinking *I am not alone.*
Instinctively she angled left and saw
A low shape moving calmly through the mud,
Nessa slowed down, peering into the fog,
And met the red eyes glowing in the dark.

"I know you," Nessa said. "Lady Possum,
Your belly must be as empty as a can
For you to be prowling so late on this grumpy night."

She matched the possum's pace. "I wish you'd speak,"
She said, "if only to explain your eyes.
How come they're red in the dark? My cat's are yellow.
What color do you see when you look at mine?"

They paralleled each other up the fence line
To the corner where the possum disappeared
In the thicket growing round the apple trees
That Nessa's people abandoned years ago.
She watched the possum burrow out of sight
And thought about the buyers moving in.
Would they have children? *Odds are they'll be improvers,*
She told herself, *removing this nest of vines*
And driving out the birds and animals;
They might break up the farm to sell off lots...,

Nessa darkened. *They might clear-cut the hill—*
Just like their neighbor down Gap Road, the one
Who never has a word for anyone
Even when spoken to. He puts down traps
For possum, stray cats, skunks, anything
That dares to live where he's put up a fence.
In Nessa's memory, hardly a week
Had passed without the stop-your-heart report
Of his rifle, and many times he'd need two rounds
(The second even worse, meaning he'd failed
To kill his victim with a single shot).

When she was younger Nessa shot a bird.
She was playing Annie Oakley. Her friend Ramon
Had handed her his Christmas BB gun.
She raised the barrel, sighting a mockingbird
On a telephone wire. "One shot," she told her friend.
Impossible. They both laughed at her bragging
As she squeezed the trigger, then the bird fell down.
Ramon picked up the rifle, ran for home,
While Nessa, unbelieving, held the bird,
Refusing to accept the death she'd made.
So that was how easy making death could be.

While Nessa walked her father sat in his chair
Between the woodstove and east-facing window.
He felt his years in the hands that held the cup,
In his heart that beat too loudly in his head.

"The bankers must hold papers on the fog
As well as the farm," he told himself. "Damn them."

A sheet of damp wood sizzled in the stove
Then blistered and exploded, arcing through
The open doors to the carpet. William was slow
To move, and in that indecisive moment
Flared a crazy thought: *The house is old,
It's possible.* But sense (or habit) prevailed.
He stamped on the ember, smiling at little burns
That scarred the carpet, a map of almost-fires.
A door creaked open, draft of cold air struck.

"It's Daddy," William said. "I'm by the fire."

Nessa kissed his cheek. He touched her hair
As she laid her head on his chest. She smelled of fog.

"You've been out walking," he said. "Did you circle the field?"

She nodded, leaning back to look at him.

"Come, red fox, be my guardian," Nessa
Whispered, as she had so many times
At bedtime when her father told her stories
Of the woods and fields. "Come, red fox, be our guide."

William turned to the woodstove saying, "Our luck's
Run out. Nothing will lift us up today."

Then Nessa's eyes were wet. She wrapped her arms
Around her father's middle from behind,
Hugging so fiercely it took him by surprise.

His power escaping like water over stone.
Like fog rolling over ditches, she thought.
They stood together, silent, sharing that touch
Until a bell ringing set them both
In motion. William hung the woodstove screen;
Nessa shook out the wheelchair's blanket and pillow
As William climbed the stairs, and moments later
Came down again, holding his wife in his arms.

※

By then the auctioneer was soaking up
A streak of egg yolk with a wedge of rye.
The banker across the table skimmed the paper,
Impatient to go. The older man could read him.

"A minute," he said, "and two more maple bars."

He signaled the waitress, requesting one more coffee
For the road. "I've got to have that kick," he said.
The banker thought of his final college term,
Living on speed as he drove toward his degree.
Now his job was easier. The figures,
The plusses and minuses bracketing his life
Made feeling a cinch; he felt the bottom line.

The auctioneer was different, a local boy
And former football star at Central Linn;
But game days in the fifties were far away.
Twice married, supporting five kids in their teens,
He specialized in liquidating estates,
Making hard times harder, talking faster
To anaesthetize the crowd's collective thought.
Foreclosures were the worst. The night before
He always felt remorse, especially
If he knew the family. But experience
Had calmed him down. The victims on sell-off day
Would suffer their greatest grief, and then go on.
(Wasn't there a famous play like that?
He couldn't recall, his reading days remote.)

It was always the same. The family
Might watch till early afternoon, then leave.

The banker's sudden question made him laugh.
"Has anybody been shot at one of these?"

He picked his teeth. The auctioneer said *no*
And asked if he had ever seen the place.

"Not me. I see it when we sell it off.
Sometimes I wish I worked home loans instead,
But that gets messy, too. You get involved,
You know what I mean? And when the loan blows up
You feel responsible. That's not for me."

                                        ❊

Nessa's mother smoothed the shawl on her legs
And stared at the fire. She drew a rattling breath
As if to say *I'm finished with this now.*

"Can I get you something, Momma?"

                                        "You've been in the field.
You saw them, then?" the older woman asked.

"I stumbled on a possum. I heard some geese,
But dark and fog were over everything.
I felt them in the shadows watching me,
But I didn't see them, no." Nessa wished
That for once she could have told a healing lie—

If only foxes carried us away,
Or wrapped a magic shawl around the farm—

She shook her head, facing the present once more,
And noticed her mother staring, far away.
"The fog has lifted a little," Nessa said.

❋

They picked at breakfast, listening to the drone
Of strangers working, setting up the yard.
The auctioneer's assistant shuffled in,
A clipboard in hand, a pencil behind one ear.

"Boss says we'll sell the tools and tractor first."

He spoke, not really to them but just to hear
a familiar sound. It kept him company.
It shielded him from the crippled woman's stare
(he felt for them, but hell, this was his job).
"Most folks are done by two o'clock," he said.
"So there's our window."
                              Nessa liked that thought—
A window that could suddenly be shut.

❋

The turn-out was good. Men were there for tools;
Women picked over tables for smaller things—
Kitchen appliances, bedding, handmade clothes,
A chair admired at a social long ago.
Nessa knew the auction etiquette,
Her family's place. Even their neighbors would turn
Away from them, keeping their hands busy.
She knew her job: to make them feel less guilty.
Embarrassing? Of course, she told herself.
She had seen her shame and loss on other faces,
On other days. Now the things they loved changed hands.
Her mother's face was stony as the quilts
She'd made sold quickly at a modest price.
Antique dealers? Nessa guessed they were.
When a batch of her mother's dresses came on the block
She turned away.
                        Out to the barn she ran.
Standing in the empty, hay-sweet place,
Which looked so big with no machinery,

She traveled back, remembering the summer
Her father and his friend had wrestled beams
Of pressure-treated lumber into place,
Restoring a foundation so delicate
It seemed a gust of wind might flatten it.
And once, while Nessa watched, the jack that held
A section up collapsed, the roof descending
Three feet or so, but holding as the two
Men in the loft yelled out in fear, then laughed
To see the roof intact, themselves alive.

But now her senses told her *look around.*
Stepping soundlessly to the rough-cut door
Of a small side room, she saw in its dusty light
Her father hauling a strongbox out of the ground.
William looked younger than she knew him to be.

It's money, enough to save us,
                                she heard him say
Though he did not speak. A raincloud covered the sun,
And in that purple light the man with his booty
Went into the air like smoke on a damp burn day.

"I'm breathing too much of this barn's old fevered air,"
She said, but there the fox stood at the door.
Then girl and animal traveled into each other
As far as they could, into the spirit's house
Where the red fox said,
                        "Into the world we're born,
Then out we're called again. Go back to your people.
They're calling you like foxes call up the night."

Then he was gone, but Nessa could hear the voice
As she ran back to the heat of the furious sale.
Her mother was already seated in the Ford
While William stood off by the oak tree with a friend.
She caught his eye, he broke free with a nod.

"I'm ready now," he said.
                        They backed away

From the house and barn, quiet in memory,
As the crowd around the auctioneer closed ranks,
Shutting them out, glad to see them going.

＊

Southwest, then west by Courtney Creek they drove,
The trailer like a pendulum behind.
They stared, not at the fields around them, but
At years behind them. The sky filled up with clouds.
A soft rain fell as William hit the lights.

They had nowhere to go, only relations
In Washington who could put them up for a spell.
They'd look for a rental, maybe a doublewide
On a farm where one or more of them could work.
William squinted, wiping at windshield mist
With the back of his sleeve.
                              "Stop!" his wife commanded.
She had seen them first, the bareheaded man and his dog
Who were walking without baggage down the road.
Perhaps the man had put his car in the ditch
And needed help, she thought. Somehow she knew
He wasn't homeless, and even if he were
What did it matter now they were homeless, too.
They slowed to a crawl, and William spoke to the man.

"It's wet out there. You'd better ride with us."

The stranger nodded, climbing in back with Nessa.
His dog, a tri-color Shelty, sat between them.
Nessa looked them over. Her first impression
Was that the man was young, but now she saw
She couldn't really tell how old he was.
The man looked fit. His eyes and face were good,
So she stroked his dog, who leaned on her for more.

"He looks a little like a fox," she said.

"That's so," the man agreed. It's then she noticed
His eyes were like the dog's, like eyes she'd seen
So many times in the fields, out in the dark.
"He's always been my guide," he said, and smiled.

Nessa's mother turned to look at them.
"It's funny you should put it that way," she said,
"Especially today." Her daughter trembled.

"So where you headed?" William's nervous eyes
In the mirror were on the stranger.
                              "Nowhere," he said.
"It doesn't really matter where I go;
What counts is how I make out while I get there.
Each day there's something new to lift us up.
Today we needed help, and there you were."

"Yes," the woman in the front seat said.
"That's how it was." She reached for William's hand
And even he could sense a change in them.
Nessa felt it, too, the silky fur
Between her fingers. The Shelty nuzzled her,
And movement out the window caught her eye.
Beyond the stranger's shoulder, in the field
She saw two foxes running easily,
Paralleling their car.
                        Then all were watching,
The dog as well, as Nessa smoothed his hair.
The foxes ran and ran until they vanished
In the longer grasses bordering the field.
At the interstate the travelers were calm,
Even grateful as they found their way.

GANDHIJI

wrinkled old man merlin of a
dream weaver boulder
the seas could not grind down
reading his thoreau
letters from tolstoy
preoccupied with precedent
custom dishonesty in the honeycomb
frail jack for the giant of empire
and doctor king seeking india
always as a pilgrim because
this was the country of gandhi

and it may be he knew this tolstoy
"I sit on a man's back
choking him and making him
carry me, and yet assure myself
and others that I am
very very sorry for him
and wish to lighten his load
by all possible means — except
by getting off his back"

but he went beyond that writer
praying for the dignity
even of oppressors
calling us out of ourselves
far from justice to that moment
with no bearings no fixed point
only the bell buoy
slipped from its moorings
clanging in the drift of the sea

HORSES IN THE LAKE

The horses go down at dawn.

They enter the golden lake and move on—
wave against wave
of arched necks and manes—
into the dazzling light.
Naked boys
bathe their haunches
   and they raise
   their antique figures,
drunk with light.
They listen,
ears attentive,
to the delicate bugle of morning,
and see
the vast battlefield.
Then they dream—
   a remote boldness
   breaks through—
soaring back
to the heroic days
when swords
returned the sun's thrusts,
white stallions
squadrons of silver
and distant cries
of birds
and wind.

But they return

   (Time
   is the whip)

With the lash
they file toward land,

heads bowed,
and yoked
  to the wagon
    the dream

remains
  behind;
    the wind's
      asleep.

trans. Grace Schulman and Ann McCarthy de Zavala

SOULS LAKE

The evergreen shadow and the pale magnolia
Stripping slowly to the air of May
Stood still in the night of the honey trees,
At rest above a star pool with my friends,
Beside that grove most fit for elegies,
I made my phrase to out-enchant the night.

The epithalamion, the hush were due,
For I had fasted and gone blind to see
What night might be beyond our passages:
Those stars so chevalier in fearful heaven
Could not but lay their steel aside and come
With a grave glitter into my low room.

Vague though the population of the earth
Lay stretched and dry below the cypresses,
It was not round-about but in my night,
Bone of my bone, as an old man would say;
And all its stone weighed my mortality;
The pool would be my body and my eyes,

The air my garment and material
Whereof that wateriness and mirror lived —
The colorable, meek and limpid world.
Though I had sworn my element alien
To the pure mind of night, the cold princes,
Behold them there, and both worlds were the same.

The heart's planet seemed not so lonely then,
Seeing what kin it found in that reclining.
And ah, though sweet the catch of your chorales,
I heard no singing there among my friends;
But still were the great waves, the lions shining,
And infinite still the discourse of the night.

PSALM #7

Yahweh, if I am to die,
let it be in the sweet scythe
of Your wood.

Rise, You who demand justice
bear Your name.
Look past intention.
Look at this face, a cooling fire,
these hands, winter leaves.

God preserves what He has pierced.

Give thanks to Yahweh,
whose voice creaks in the starry wood,
the whole place alive somehow
with water. Heavy grasses, green,
dark with it, and I feel the
same night the foliage does,
recite the same verses.
My body, too, belongs to the great
material curve of this planet, sky.
It is who I am, this way and
terminus. It haunts my every
blind and faithful step with the
signature of what we are, the promise
of where we live.

GOD

Numbers from one to ten, however, are called
"God." In other words, counting to ten you would
say, "God, God, God, God, God, God, God, God, God,
God." It is possible to distinguish among these
numbers by the tone in which each is pronounced.
"God," for example, corresponding to our "five,"
is pitched relatively high on the musical scale,
and accordingly sounds an inquisitive, even plaintive,
note. It is in sharp contrast to the number corre-
sponding to our "ten," which has a slightly accented,
basso finality, thus: "God."

January 19: St. Anthony of the Desert

ON HEARING GREGORIAN CHANT
IN THE ABBEY OF SOLESMES

When I visited the Monks of Solesmes
and heard them intone the Plain Chant
we used to sing when I was a novice,
I felt as if an old friend sat again
beside me, a welcome guest now that we
modern friars wake to the Morning News.

No bells, no "Deo Gratias" to answer
a brother's "Benedicite" as he knocks
passing down the corridor. We still
meditate, but seldom together; Mass
and morning office come after coffee
breaking an antique Eucharistic fast.

Daily newspapers clutter our tables
where we talk and eat the ordinary.
We wear jeans and shirts and sweaters.
Not that Chant and religious habits,
Latin and the Magnum Silentium,
create what monks and friars long for:

but something is discordant.
We need what Chant evokes, a rhythm
learned, handed down—grace of continuity,
danger of routine—the ancient tension of
brothers before us who chanted, fasted,
found vision (or sloth) in silent meditation.

THE MONASTERY GATE

I

The crickets had gone underground. Pax intrantibus:
the stone arch stood an implacable sentry.
The Guest Master came by, yawning in the sunlight.

"O God, come to my assistance," the chorister intoned.
The final Psalm went flat. The bowed heads rose
into the recessional of heavy robes.

Oblong, almond-eyed, Mary's icon remained.

In the guest house lobby, St. Anthony trudged
through the desert with all his demons in tow.
No one was excluded from those hallways,
not even the most devout of the demons.

What can a person vowed to silence do
when the most convinced must lose their way?

II

Brother Giles squinted in the courtyard. The trees
surrounded us like exquisite axioms. In the distance

a runner was climbing a hill,
passing a concubine lumbering beside the road.

Smiling like he saw jokes on the trees, Brother Giles said,
"If you want to be a monk, don't be so scrupulous;
it isn't being very kind to God."

Soon he would chant more Psalms in the church.

He said, "It's the biggest bunch of noise I've ever heard."

THE TRAPPIST ABBEY: MATINS

(our Lady of Gethsemani, Kentucky)

When the full fields begin to smell of sunrise
And the valleys sing in their sleep,
The pilgrim moon pours over the solemn darkness
Her waterfalls of silence,
And then departs, up the long avenue of trees.

The stars hide, in the glade, their light, like tears,
And tremble where some train runs, lost,
Baying in eastward mysteries of distance,
Where fire flares, somewhere, over a sink of cities.

Now kindle in the windows of this ladyhouse, my soul,
Your childish, clear awakeness:
Burn in the country night
Your wise and sleepless lamp.
For, from the frowning tower, the windy belfry,
Sudden the bells come, bridegrooms,
And fill the echoing dark with love and fear.

Wake in the windows of Gethsemani, my soul, my sister,
For the past years, with smokey torches, come,
Bringing betrayal from the burning world
And bloodying the glade with pitch flame.

Wake in the cloisters of the lonely night, my soul, my sister,
Where the apostles gather, who were, one time, scattered,
And mourn God's blood in the place of His betrayal,
And weep with Peter at the triple cock-crow.

EVENING: ZERO DEGREE WEATHER

Now the lone world is streaky as a wall of marble
With veins of clear and frozen snow.
There is no bird-song there, no hare's track
No badger working in the russet grass:
All the bare fields are silent as eternity.

And the whole herd is home in the long barn.
The brothers come, with hoods about their faces,
Following their plumes of breath
Lugging the gleaming buckets one by one.

This was a day when shovels would have struck
Full flakes of fire out of the land like rock:
And ground cries out like iron beneath our boots

When all the monks come in with eyes as clean as the cold sky
And axes under their arms,
Still paying out Ave Marias
With rosaries between their bleeding fingers.

We shake the chips out of our robes outside the door
And go to hide in cowls as deep as clouds,
Bowing our shoulders in the church's shadow, lean and whipped,
To wait upon your Vespers, Mother of God!

And we have eyes no more for the dark pillars or the freezing windows,
Ears for the rumorous cloister or the chimes of time above our heads:
For we are sunken in the summer of our adoration,
And plunge, down, down into the fathoms of our secret joy
That swims with indefinable fire.

And we will never see the copper sunset
Linger a moment, like an echo, on the frozen hill
Then suddenly die an hour before the Angelus.
For we have found our Christ, our August

Here in the zero days before Lent—
We are already binding up our sheaves of harvest
Beating the lazy liturgy, going up with exultation
Even on the eve of our Ash Wednesday,
And entering our blazing heaven by the doors of the Assumption!

WINTER AFTERNOON

Who shall bridle the winds, in their seven directions,
(Now from the north, now from the livid east)
Worrying again these birdless branches,
Storming our forests from the dark south, or the west?

We are within the wild doors of another winter
And the black cedars, bowing in the sleet
Sigh all their incoherent music to the tuneless country
Waking the deep wood's muffled antiphons.
Walking among the sleepless, iron cemetery crosses,
We praise you, winter, from the deck
Of this our lonely Abbey like an anchored battleship:

While the Kentucky forest
Pouring upon our prows her rumorous seas
Wakes our wordless prayers with the soft din of an Atlantic.

And we look up and praise you, winter,
And think of time and the uncertain centuries
Flying before your armies like the coward sky.

And oh! From some far rock some echo of your iron, December,
Halts our slow steps, and calls us to the armored parapet
Searching the flying skyline for some glare of prophecy.

We thought we heard John-Baptist or Elias, there, on the dark hill
Or else the angel with the trumpet of the Judgement.

AGAINST INTRUSION

When my friend drove up the mountain
it changed itself into a big
lump of land with lots of snow on it
and slopes of arid scree.
Another friend climbed it the hard way:
exciting to stay the course, get to the top —
but no sense of height there, nothing to see but
generic mist and snow.
As for me,
when my photos come back developed,
there's just the lake, the south shore of the lake,
the middle distance. No mountain.
            How clearly it speaks! *Respect, perspective,*
privacy, it teaches. *Indulgence*
of curiosity increases
ignorance of the essential.
What does it serve to insist
on knowing more than that a mountain,
forbearing — so far — from volcanic rage,
blesses the city it is poised above, angelic guardian
at rest on sustaining air; and that its vanishings
are needful, as silence is to music?

January 20: St. Sebastian

SEBASTIAN, THE SAINT

Nearly haloed in chalk, quivering
      he wonders if he arose
from this gutter and responded to the cue
of the stalk creeping steadily up through
the dung heap, could he acquire
      the faith or the pose
he'd neglected, caking on their hearts
      like a stain no hose
could take up, nor dog's tongue lap? But who

will be relieved by this present portrait? What few
pass him by have been spooned out the same dose
of hardship, sputtering towards the abyss, jamming
the gateway with drive-shafts and fenders,
a collection of bones dyed
with bargain-black repentance and stacked up
      like pre-packaged yokes.

Only the Rain can be believed—
exile enhanced by the sky's leaden lungs,
      its thunderous slamming
of doors, while even his memory is kicked
      into the shadows or applied to their
wounds like a finger that provokes.

January 28: St. Thomas Aquinas

AQUINAS PERCHED
(IN VITERBO PERCHED)

Seven hundred and more years ago—

>   so that the people could have
>   the very sky above them
>   when the Preachers preached

an ambo was fixed
>   outside
high up along the wall of the church

where a fat and holy man could climb and cry
>   "Repent!"
And then the message would not sting so strong

because all the birds and the sun on the stones of the square
(so beautiful, so light, so fair)
would be there offering their own obedience to nature's ways
and add their tones to the preacher's pleas.

The trees could bend to the Gospel's breeze
and everything everywhere invite everyone
>   to bend toward Grace
>   to be bathed in Grace
>   to fly upward toward Grace.

ORDINARY TIME

February 23: St. Polycarp

STROLLING FROM THE DELI,
GROCERY-LADEN

A new generation rises through us
without the will or luck or assistance to *thrive:*
    psychologists, politicians, educators
argue incapable intellectualizations —
    deviancy & lack of character, blahblah.
I've tipped my idols, butchered my sacred
cows, made some concomitant progress
to parenthood. Still, the statue-sellers cry
"what's wrong with them?"
as our youth continue to die, daily.

    On the beach gate my daughters
have hung blue crabs for decoration,
green flies swarm the feast. More pleasant
are the bees in flowers, our old goat coughing,
the wap-wap! of wind under a nylon kite.
As I pass, the fly-blown crabs rattle.
Waves detonate on Haystack Rock
louder than my neighbor's shotgun.
    He cries pull! and his son
    launches another clay pigeon.

Fortunately, I burned the mortgage
on this paradise before I was downsized.
But *them*? Our children? We think we are safe
here — stroll from the deli, grocery-laden.

19TH-CENTURY TRAVELER
ON THE RIO SAN JUAN

The silent bungo was oared up the river
bordered by water lilies and rushes
                    (as wide as the Seine in front of the Louvre).
The birds quit singing,
and all was quietness and endless verdure and echoless retreats.
At 6 o'clock night came without twilight.
Only the plash of oars in the river was heard...
And my thoughts filled with shadows,
        and I fell asleep.

When I awoke the bungo was motionless in the dark.
We were tied up to the trunk of a tree.
Thousands of fireflies in the black foliage
and the Southern Cross
deep in the black sky...
And there was a clamor in the air:
the cry perhaps of a strange bird,
answering another cry like it farther off.
Sarapiquí!:
The water so clear
it was invisible.
Two green riverbanks
        and the riverbanks upside down.
Blue sky above
                    and sky below.
And the water in between, invisible.

NEWS REPORT, SEPTEMBER 1991
U.S. BURIED IRAQI SOLDIERS
ALIVE IN GULF WAR

"What you saw was a
bunch of trenches with
arms sticking out."
"Plows mounted on
tanks. Combat
earthmovers."
"Defiant."
"Buried."
"Carefully planned and
rehearsed."
"When we
went through there wasn't
anybody left."
"Awarded
Silver Star."
"Reporters
banned."
"Not a single
American killed."
"Bodycount
impossible."
"For all I know,
thousands, said
Colonel Moreno."
"What you
saw was a bunch of
buried trenches
with people's
arms and things
sticking out."
"Secretary Cheney
made no mention."
"Every single American
was inside

the juggernaut
impervious
to small-arms
fire." *"I know
burying people
like that sounds
pretty nasty,* said
Colonel Maggart,
But..."
"His force buried
about six hundred
and fifty
in a thinner line
of trenches."
*"People's arms
sticking out."*
"Every American
inside."
"The juggernaut."
*"I'm not
going to sacrifice
the lives
of my soldiers,*
Moreno said, *it's not
cost-effective."*
*"The tactic was designed
to terrorize,*
Lieutenant Colonel Hawkins
said, who helped
devise it."
"Schwartzkopf's staff
privately
estimated fifty to seventy
thousand killed
in the trenches."
"Private Joe Queen was
awarded
a Bronze Star for burying
trenches with his
earthmover."

"Inside
the juggernaut."
"Impervious."
A lot of the guys
were scared, he said,
but I
enjoyed it."
"A bunch of
trenches. People's
arms and things
sticking out."
"Cost-effective."

SUPPLICATIONS TO THE BLESSED MOTHER

All evening the furnace spun its woolly heat
and the dull pendulum swung.
Sleeping in bloodless sheets, I dreamt
the bedclothes had been stripped and burned,
and I had sewn my own lips together,
stitched my eyelids shut.
It was then that you came to me —
a kind-eyed lady at my window,
a loose grace caught
in the chicken wire of my dreams.

In the kitchen the curtains leak vanilla light
as I lick burnt sugar from each fingertip,
hoping to find them pricked by some dread
spindle, the visitation of night.
What hope is in a rotten apple to be cored
or a rusty pot brought to boil?

Sturdy sunflowers gossip in the ditch,
thrive along the section road,
but my garden is sparse
and the rain will not come.
Holy Mary, in your mercy,
hear and answer me.

Sometimes I sleep on burlap and damp hay
and wake to the rafters of the barn,
to all the pails of cream spilt in the dirt
and the thick milk bottles broken.

I stare up at the swallows skeining our sorrow
and know that what I desire, I do not deserve.
But always my prayers get trapped
between these teeth
and this clabbered tongue.

Take away the stone
from my throat and loosen
my knotted breath.
Forgive me for all
I have not done.
I'll shake the cornsilk from my skirts
and go out to meet the day.

I want to push a cart across the countryside,
barefoot and blithe,
peddling shoe polish and shining pots
to farmers and their wives.
I'd call out my love of vegetables,
the virtue of radish and cabbage,
and the beauty of tomatoes tight in their skins.
I want bounty to sprout from the cracks of my palms,
grace to gather in these hands.

I dream split pods lay at my feet
and peas roll off my fingers,
tumble into my lap.
I dream of a table's plenty
and the platter passed steaming, heavy,
heavy hangs over my head.
I dream I feed a baby rhubarb leaves.
This child is me.

Sleep and wake; dream and speak;
Seed and rind; pulp and vine.
Give us peace, mother and moon,
mother of us all.

February 23: St. Polycarp

POLYCARP

the city of smyrna
bosnia of its day
and wherever else
our murderous desires are

better not to know
nuances of hate or the cruel
need to preserve a self
down a hundred generations

better remember the victim
his shattering
his bodys sharing

his prayer for us

he was the incandescent man
an oven as they said of him
his death fire his sheath until
his captors broke his heart with a spear
and his agony turned to ashes

his hallmark was forgiveness
they came for him in darkness
it was long toward midnight
and so he gave them wine

and he fed them

ASH WEDNESDAY

THE LITANY

This is a litany of lost things,
a canon of possessions dispossessed,
a photograph, an old address, a key.
It is a list of words to memorize
or to forget — of *amo, amas, amat,*
the conjugations of a dead tongue
in which the final sentence has been spoken.

This is the liturgy of rain,
falling on mountain, field, and ocean —
indifferent, anonymous, complete —
of water infinitesimally slow,
sifting through rock, pooling in darkness,
gathering in springs, then rising without our agency,
only to dissolve in mist or cloud or dew.

This is a prayer to unbelief,
to candles guttering and darkness undivided,
to incense drifting into emptiness.
It is the smile of a stone madonna
and the solar fury of the consecrated wine,
a benediction on the death of a young god,
brave and beautiful, rotting on a tree.

This is a litany to earth and ashes,
to the dust of roads and vacant rooms,
to the fine silt circling in a shaft of sun,
settling indifferently on books and beds.
This is a prayer to praise what we become,
"Dust thou art, to dust thou shalt return."
Savor its taste — the bitterness of earth and ashes.

This is a prayer, inchoate and unfinished,
for you, my love, my loss, my lesion,
a rosary of words to count out time's
illusions, all the minutes, hours, days
the calendar compounds as if the past

existed somewhat—like an inheritance
still waiting to be claimed.

Until at last it is our litany, *mon vieux*,
my reader, my voyeur, as if the mist
steaming from the gorge, this pure paradox,
the shattered river rising as it falls—
splintering the light, swirling it skyward,
neither transparent nor opaque but luminous,
even as it vanishes—were not our life.

STUDY IN BLACK & WHITE
For Flannery, who showed the way, on her seventieth

Seven days a week, six till ten,
my father & I ran the Sinclair station
across from the county courthouse in Mineola.
Between customers I pored over *The Greatest
Story Ever Told* and *Amboy Dukes*

or worked out back among the jewelweed
& cinders, swabbing ball bearings in kerosene,
as I gloried in all I would in time become.
Late April and early May, and the trees trembling
for the sun's caress. Hummed the papers

daily now of the noose growing tighter
round Dien Bien Phu. Black & white photos,
ghostly, dreamlike, with black-pajammed Viet
Minh sappers storming trenches as elite
French paratroopers began surrendering in droves.

I was fourteen and stood ready
to take on evil wherever it might rear
its ugly head, like the Archangel Michael
whose eight-foot statue hovered high above
the marblewhite high altar of Corpus Christi.

Armored like the young Augustus Imperator,
his bronze spear stirred the snarling serpent.
Only Butch, who lived behind the diner
two doors up in his '41 woodtrimmed Chevy
wagon up on blocks, seemed not to care

that the world my father'd helped make safe
was already breaking down. Butch spent
his days poring over comics, small ones, black
& white, in which Wimpy did forbidden things
to Olive. In all weathers, buried beneath

a filthy army-issue blanket flanked by whisky
flasks & stacks of yellowed newsprint, his palsied
body shook. But who knew anything about him really?
Where he came from or later where he went?
My father warned me to keep away from him,

and when I asked him why, stared down at me
in utter disbelief. Could any son of his
be that fucking stupid & still walk upright
the face of God's sweet earth? That was forty
years ago, so that by now Butch has surely

gone back to the same dust from which we all
once sprang, his end coming in some alley,
or one fine morning not waking from the backseat
of his car, monoxide leaking into his final
dream of love to resurface here defanged:

thinning hair slicked back, the toothless grin,
the right hand grasping the palsied left
to hide the shaking as he sized you up, a face
I would recognize in any bathroom mirror,
the poor forked mortal trembling thing itself.

ONE WORD

I have in my throat one word
that I cannot speak, will not free
though its thrust of blood pounds me.
If I voiced it, it would scorch the living grass,
bleed the lamb, fell the bird.

I have to cut it from my tongue,
find a beaver's hole,
or bury it beneath lime and more quicklime
lest, soul-like, it break free.

I wish to give no sign of what I live
as this word courses through my blood, ebbs and flows,
rises, falls with each mad breath.
Though Job, my father, burning, spoke it,
I will not give it utterance
lest it roll vagrant
and be found by river-women,
twist itself in their braids,
or mangle and blaze the poor thicket.

I wish to throw seeds so violent
they burst and smother it in one night
leaving not even a syllable's trace.
Or rip it from myself
with the serpent's severing tooth.

And return to my house, enter and sleep,
torn from it, sliced from it;
wake after two thousand days
newly born out of sleep and oblivion.

Never again to remember the word between my lips,
that word of iodine and alum stone,

or ever again that one night,
the ambush in a foreign land,
the lightning bolt at the door
and my flesh abroad with no soul.

translated by Doris Dana

LENT

REQUIESCAT FOR A MATADOR

Come, Dominguin, arise,
your wars with that trinity
of snort, horn, and hoof
were won ages ago. Bloody
blots on pastel tunics
the charlatans wore afternoons
into Madrid's arena never slashed
yours open to a crucifix's
self-assured glimmer. Zinnias
kissed your scarlet cape
making such a specter of misses.
Your swivel hips drew
a slight sword dealing death's swift
but sweetly incisive amen.
Yet long after the sunlit bleachers
faded to a medieval murk — Hemingway
shot to Idaho, Ava left a weeping
beauty, Picasso undressed
to brush abstraction — you tumbled
to green sawdust, gored deep down
to the guts with cancer's
bullish point on yesterday's glitz.

CORNICHE

I work all day and hardly drink at all.
I can reach down and feel if I'm depressed.
I adore the Creator because I made myself
and a few times a week a wire jags in my chest.

The first time, I'd been coming apart all year,
weeping, incoherent; cigars had given me up;
any road round a cliff edge I'd whimper along in low gear
then: cardiac horror. Masking my pulse's calm lub-dub.

It was the victim-sickness. Adrenalin howling in my head,
the black dog was my brain. Come to drown me in my breath
was energy's black hole, depression, compere of the predawn show
when, returned from a pee, you stew and welter in your death.

The rogue space rock is on course to snuff your world,
sure. But go acute, and its oncoming fills your day.
The brave die but once? I could go a hundred times a week,
clinging to my pulse with the world's edge inches away.

Laugh, who never shrank around wizened genitals there
or killed themselves to stop dying. The blow that never falls
batters you stupid. Only gradually do
you notice a slight scorn in you for what appalls.

A self inside self, cool as conscience, one to be erased
in your final night, or faxed, still knows beneath
all the mute grand opera and uncaused effect —
that death which can be imagined is not true death.

The crunch is illusion. There's still no outside world
but you start to see. You're like one enthralled by bad art —
yet for a real onset, what cover! You gibber to Casualty,
are checked, scorned, calmed. There's nothing wrong with your heart.

The terror of death is not afraid of death.
Fear, pure, is intransitive. A Hindenburg of vast rage

rots, though, above your life. See it, and you feel flogged
but like an addict you sniffle aboard, to your cage,

because you will cling to this beast as it gnaws you,
for the crystal in its kidneys, the elixir in its wings,
till your darlings are the police of an immense fatigue.
I came to the world unrehearsed but I've learned some things.

When you curl, stuffed, in the pot at rainbow's end
it is life roaring and racing and nothing you can do.
Were you really God you could have lived all the lives
that now decay into misery and cripple you.

A for adrenalin, the original A-bomb, fuel
and punishment of aspiration, the Enlightenment's air-burst.
Back when God made me, I had no script. It was better.
For all the death, we also die unrehearsed.

MAGNUM XL-200

Cedar Point, Ohio

For maximum speed, he rode the Magnum
fully loaded at 3:13, the hottest time
of the day. It ripped, from its crest, down the 195
feet at 60° and 73 miles per hour—
at 3.55 g, like the turns at Indy.
Two minutes later, he couldn't get out of the car,
sitting helpless, pale and suffocated,
listening to his strange arrhythmic heart.

Sure it was embarrassing: an overweight, middle-
aged man who spent his vacations riding roller coasters.
But he didn't care. The panic distracted his mind
from his boring job, the inconsiderate wife,
and their whacked-out, dropped-out, wise-assed, teenage sons.
So he'd never even mentioned the mitral valve prolapse.
If it happened, it happened, which, five months later, it did,
On the Coney Island Cyclone, a mile from home.

RUNWAY

Was it really her he saw last night?
Sitting in a limousine on 67th
Street near Tavern on the Green?
Expressionless, yet just as beautiful
as twenty years ago, when he'd pursued her
at the Jersey shore. Until one night
she said, "All right," and took him to the airport
at two A.M. and climbed beneath the fence.

Then, side by side, they lay down in a ditch
in front of Runway 12. She held him close,
and then he saw it, huge, with flashing lights,
descending from the sky, like a bird of prey,
tremendous, closer, falling down upon them,
then roaring over their heads onto the runway —
and she looked into his eyes, as if to say,
"*This* is what life with me is like!"

FROM

THE EASTERN POINT MEDITATIONS

IT WAS DURING THIS TIME THAT A SERIOUS DISTURBANCE BROKE
OUT IN CONNECTION WITH THE WAY. A SILVERSMITH CALLED
DEMETRIUS, WHO EMPLOYED A LARGE NUMBER OF CRAFTSMEN
MAKING SILVER SHRINES OF DIANA, CALLED A MEETING OF HIS
OWN MEN WITH OTHERS IN THE SAME TRADE. "AS YOU MEN
KNOW," HE SAID, "IT IS ON THIS INDUSTRY THAT WE DEPEND FOR
OUR PROSPERITY. NOW YOU MUST HAVE SEEN AND HEARD HOW,
NOT JUST IN EPHESUS BUT NEARLY EVERYWHERE IN ASIA, THIS
MAN PAUL HAS PERSUADED AND CONVERTED A GREAT NUMBER
OF PEOPLE WITH HIS ARGUMENT THAT GODS MADE BY HAND
ARE NOT GODS AT ALL. THIS THREATENS NOT ONLY TO DIS-
CREDIT OUR TRADE, BUT ALSO TO REDUCE THE SANCTUARY OF
THE GREAT GODDESS DIANA TO UNIMPORTANCE. IT COULD END
UP BY TAKING AWAY ALL THE PRESTIGE OF A GODDESS VENER-
ATED ALL OVER ASIA, YES, AND EVERYWHERE IN THE CIVILIZED
WORLD."

—ACTS, 19:23-28.

WE ARE ALWAYS WILLING TO FANCY OURSELVES WITHIN A
LITTLE OF HAPPINESS AND WHEN, WITH REPEATED EFFORTS WE
CANNOT REACH IT, PERSUADE OURSELVES THAT IT IS INTER-
CEPTED BY AN ILL-PAIRED MATE SINCE, IF WE COULD FIND ANY
OTHER OBSTACLE, IT WOULD BE OUR OWN FAULT THAT IT WAS
NOT REMOVED.

—DR. JOHNSON

i.
November 5th: Monday night

In shadow, in late light breaking only now
beneath the piled clouds behind me, a milksoft
moon before me lifting, nearly full and pale, bluepurple
and translucent wafer, heaven's bread suspended

as I raced east along the northern route,
straining to read the dark lines of the map
beside me in the empty seat, intent upon a silence
ripped jagged by the sweep of rigs and the patter

of unsteady rain, towards the Eastern Point
retreat house and so away as quickly as I could
from lives I'd left in shambles, not knowing
even now how little I had known myself

or my wolf-fanged lust for doe flank, breast & vulva,
not even caring this time round that I was leaving
what had taken twenty years to build, having kept
guard over my mate & three mancubs day in day out

with an angry jealous fevered eye, a half-crazed timberwolf
loping through a silverdrunken moonscape out now wholly
for himself. I caught the flash of nippled globe & buttock
fleeing in the headlights as I entered Gloucester,

searching for the lighthouse. *If you want the desert,*
for God's sake go alone, my oldest son had stuttered
through clenched teeth, embarrassed for the man he called
his father, streaked cheeks glinting from the lights there

in the highschool parking lot, the neutral ground
I'd chosen where I thought I could "explain." And now,
alone in dark again, past shrouded houses and the waters
all about me, in silent, fumbling prayer, the buzzing

honeysuckle scent of estrus still about me,
I groped my way back through clamant foghorns
and the rise & fall of harbor bells to try & piece together
the world I'd lifted high to smash against the rocks.

GHOST

After so much time you think
you'd have it netted
in the mesh of language. But again
it reconfigures, slick as Proteus.

You're in the kitchen talking
with your ex-Navy brother, his two kids
snaking over his tattooed arms, as he goes on
& on about being out of work again.

For an hour now you've listened,
his face growing dimmer in the lamplight
as you keep glancing at your watch
until it's there again: the ghost rising

as it did that first time when you,
the oldest, left home to marry.
You're in the boat again, alone, and staring
at the six of them, your sisters

& your brothers, their faces bobbing
in the water, as their fingers grapple
for the gunwales. The ship is going down,
your mother with it. One oar's locked

and feathered, and one oar's lost,
there's a slop of gurry pooling
in the bottom, and your tiny boat
keeps drifting further from them.

Between each bitter wave you can count
their upturned faces — white roses
scattered on a mash of sea, eyes fixed
to see what you will do. And you?

You their old protector, you their guardian
and go-between? Each man for himself,
you remember thinking, their faces
growing dimmer with each oarstroke.

IN RETREAT

1

To stop in the ascending triangle
of an unknown face
after midnight when
shadows turn into their reverse
and silence grows organic as a star;

to lay down on the forehead's sand,
to rest upon the eyebrows' shadow
and to watch the green waves below
on the surging sea of the pupils;

and to get formulated in the silence
as a needed self-legitimation,
as there's a more complete reality,
a self-suggestion that's more creditable.

2

To stop in the crib-smelling warmth
of an unknown face
and to tiptoe and peep in through
the loop-hole window of devotion:

you can see him in the innermost room
where rowdy clamour can't penetrate
nor rude noises nor babies' shrieks
and Herodean curses;

to walk across the glass hall
groping your way in the widening darkness
towards the last of battles lost
where there are no more victors and defeated.

3

To stop in the volley of judgment
from an unknown face
impersonally in the end,
to shoulder a more perfect
nativity, the faith of a newborn babe;

then to set off
and to wander on unflinching
in search of that cleft
through which the bloodhounds of fear
disappear when you wake.

PSALM #6

Do not punish me, do not
stamp my soul with the seal
of who I am.
Lift me up and I will rise,
pity me, I cannot keep
my bones, the rack
upon which I starve, knit.

Come back, rescue me.
This is what You do.

I could sing Your praises
in the lands of the dead,
but who would hear me?
Take these hands, lifted;
a person follows.

I am worn out with groaning,
my enemies, younger each year,
surround me.

Yahweh calls me back
as he always has,
with the sound of trumpets,
the breaking of expected days.

I come,
in human skin.

ENGLISH NIGHT

No more resolutions, Lord,
No long-term plans, or visions
Of what might be —
These only come between us.
No offering you my heart now,
You've shown me what it is —
Wastrel seeking waste,
Selling itself to any bidder
Offering comfort's moment.
It, too, traitor's emissary,
Will block the way to you.
I have only a cry now
Rising from parched places,
And the sword of memory
When — for a moment — my head rested
On your breast.
Even this will not suffice,
For all that is mine
Turns and strikes poison,
Thrusting in the lance.
Your wounds have not dried up, Lord,
They flow the more, as if
In parched diminishment to give
Voice, heart, eyes for one
In this night's groping still
Seeking father's welcome.

(ONE BIRD)

one   two   three   one
bird   birds   birds

one   two   four   one
                birds

PALM SUNDAY

PRELUDE TO HOLY WEEK

At the end of every sonnet, where flawed
Rhyme schemes fail and iambs crumble
Into sultry silence, there is a breathless
Waiting, a spark of a wish that God
Might have spoken through the old, weary forms.
But who am I kidding—myself? God?
A few patient friends receiving stuffed envelopes?
The nub of it all is: I got stripped,
Rubbed to the raw, till the wounds gaped
And flowed, and now nothing will staunch it.
I am like a bird driven crazy by contrary winds,
Flying back and forth between lost worlds.
One minute I agree to my assigned role:
Gently, to father a multitude. Instantly depleted,
I am then a heat-seeking adolescent, craving
Warmth and the comfort of the gang—fatherless, lost.
And who sees the difference between one and the other?
Only God's all-seeing eye gazes steadily,
And does not look away disgusted—this I know.
Poetry is a failure, I am no true father
But only a poor coward, lamely smiling.
Another day or so, we'll sing, "Hosanna"
To the Failure-King riding his donkey of peace.
And I want to say, choking back sobs,
"Hosanna. I still want to try. Blessed be He who comes."
I have no other hope, yet I seek still
False hopes, and I am afraid, afraid
Of committing some definitive sickly betrayal.
The last gut of courage has drained away,
And only you can be resurrection in it all.
Hosanna. Make a kingdom of this dust.

March 1997

GOOD FRIDAY

SILVER AGE

A Silver age. Words get lost
Sentences are lost. Their vaults
break in and collapse
burying the talking skulls of the past
underneath them.

A Bone. A heap of bones.
On the swelling hills' violent
Spring scatters those on
its way: They have grown
thinner, porous organic sieve
hip, shoulder, and jawbones

This is the hill of skulls
crossless contours growing
underneath and inside them
day by day self-wasting silence
drives itself into the deep
with increasing intensity

You said: it is the fate of all
the skeleton of crumpled words
obstinately receding towards
an imaginary center
in thickening clumps.

In the middle all is still
Even if sounding, words don't spread out
A balance is guarded in it
by the paternal source of a different language:

but never in words about that

APPROACHING SLEEP

Footsteps in the attic, those crooked sounds
You hear at night, the train's blind whistle or
Dead letters slipped beneath your bedroom door,

And still there is your heart that beats upon
Your ear and fills you as you lie in bed;
It beats and beats but cannot keep good time

And lets it drip like water from a tap.
You write a letter of complaint to God
While half asleep, forgetting the address.

Outside, the night is wide as a winter lake
After the heavy rains, and it is June
With days that open like a Chinese box.

If anything is real it is the mind
Approaching sleep, listing the tiny bones
Within the ear: anvil, stirrup, hammer...

The surgeon placed them on a woman's watch,
The seconds crudely sweeping underneath.
Within the ear, a fine Dutch miniature

With cool canals, a blacksmith by his horse,
A small boy playing on a smaller drum,
Old women who darn their shadows again each dusk.

There is a monster in the labyrinth
But still behind you, walking when you walk:
It is too late to get out now, the watch

You hold up to your ear stopped long ago;
That angry letter you wrote to God returns
Addressed to you, but now means something else.

CRUOR DEI

As if we arrived through the blind extremes
of sleep, we opened our mouths, eyes closed,
and the priest laid on our tongues his coins
of bread, what we learned never to cross
with our teeth, never to rush, for at the heart
of each was God's nerve, burning and alive.

Then we washed it down with wine and Latin—
cruor dei, God's blood, the stuff I figured
flowed in everyone's body—what did I know—
though here was the glad horror of appetite
taking it in, and memories of other gods,
how they in their stories were torn apart,

exploding into the ten thousand things,
into the still conscious body of names
for things, with every word a hint of blood.
It's how I picture crowning into the world,
through the red water over rims of bone
into a little chaos of lights and gasping.

I like to think the blade binds as it cuts,
mother from child, that each solitude
ripens into a name for the other.
And as the mother looks down, her voice
is a braid of scar tissue between them.
It draws the child further into debt

he never resolves, not wholly, but sees
in the unlikely bodies of passersby,
in the man, say, caught on film, who keeps
bending back the car door, pulling a stranger
from a seat on fire—a birth of sorts,
though none is entirely his to repay.

It's only the trace, at best, a kindness
remade the way gods remake themselves

in our image, half-naked, their hands nailed
to some bare wall in sweltering Texas.
Their feet are vines crossing in the brick shade.
They would turn us all into mothers, grieving.

And among our children: debt and hunger.
Sometimes you feel them thinking, confiding
in the barely audible speech of twins.
In bad times they almost sound like hope.
Which they are. So many cuts, so many streams
of erotic letters welling up in the rift:

a lover says goodbye in the hazard lights
of an idling taxi, a pulse in the eye
she will never quite remember nor forget,
not completely, and to live just this side
of completion is to turn further inward
the way a key of light turns in a gaze.

So it is with my father in his illness,
railing at the bolted apartment door,
cursing his wife for locking up his wife.
Or swearing he is the doctor again
with patients enthralled in another room.
He is the complicated child, the latch

lifting on an intricate cage. He scissors us
into broken flocks of memory and wish
which are his own body tearing apart,
though it is tough to say he suffers
the knowledge, our sense of what he was
or will be. It could be kindness too:

the bony dice of days stumbling through him,
the bewildering children who hold out
their shadowy bruises, too young to know
which wounds are serious—they all seem so
early on—or which ones simply clear up
with time, going clean in their own blood.

A MEAL NOW AND THEN

Elegy for the friend of a friend

We almost sat at table once,
but the cards could not be dealt.
A storm arose, or a plane was missed,
something.

So we never knew if we'd be friends;
having a friend in common is
of course no guarantee.

When she learned the diagnosis,
she asked my prayers and so
for the last years I prayed
for some one I might never meet.

The case is settled now.
The disposition is clear,
as definitive as the body
brought down from the cross.

What did the friends think,
having left Jesus wrapped
in cloth away from their eyes
forever, they thought, in the tomb?

Never again to see,
never again to hear the voice
of one they loved.

I have known this silent stone,
rolled over the mouth of death.
I have seen the lid sealed
over the remains of father, grandparents,
friends. I have awaited the day
of my children, when they will arise
in the embrace of their ancestors.

For what are we waiting, my loved ones,
here on the edge of this world
that to us does not seem a horizon?

The horizon is always beyond us.
There the sun rises, the moon too.
There the sun sinks.
                Yet we wait,
expecting the Last Day, here

which to the Holy Fire that is coming
is the edge of a darkness
that will be transformed.

We wait, the long trial of waiting,
the sentence incomplete.

Will we be filled with the fire?
What will be the banquet
when horizons cease?
Will we find ourselves
at the same table at last?

My friend says so.

She has arranged the table
many times. We have
eaten with her before.

Why should we not
feast together again
then?

FINAL TREE

This solitary fretwork
they gave me at birth
that goes from side
to fiery side,

that runs from my forehead
to my hot feet,
this island of my blood
this minuteness of kingdom

I return it fulfilled.
With arms outstretched I give it
to the last of my trees,
to tamarinth or cedar.

In case in the second life
they will not give again what has been given
and I should miss this solace
of freshness and silence,

and if I should pass through the world
in dream, running or flying,
instead of thresholds of houses
I shall want a tree to rest under.

I bequeath it all I had
of ash and firmament,
my flank of speech,
my flank of silence.

Loneliness I gave myself,
loneliness they gave me,
the small tithe I paid the lightning
of my God, sweet and tremendous.

My play of give and take
with clouds and with the winds

and what I knew, trembling,
of secret springs.

Ay! Tremulous shelter
of my true Archangel,
ahead on every road
with branch and balsam.

Perhaps it is already born
and I lack the grace to know it,
or it was that nameless tree
I carried like a blind son.

At times a dampness falls
around my shoulders, a soft breeze,
and I see about me
the girdle of my tree.

Perhaps its foliage
already clothes my dream
and in death I sing beneath it
without knowing.

translated by Doris Dana

THE ROOM UPSTAIRS

Come over to the window for a moment—
I want to show you something. Do you see
The one hill without trees? The dust-brown one
Above the highway? That's how it all looked
When I first came—no watered lawns or trees,
Just open desert, pale green in the winter,
Then brown and empty till the end of fall.
I never look in mirrors anymore,
Or if I do I just stare at the tie
I'm knotting, and it's easy to pretend
I haven't changed. But how can I ignore
The way these hills were cut up into houses?
I always thought the desert would outlive me.

How did I get started on this subject?
I'm really not as morbid as I sound.
We hardly know each other, but I think
You'll like it here—the college isn't far,
And this old house, like me, still has its charms.
I chose the site myself and drew the plans—
A modern house, all open glass and stone,
The rooms squared off and cleared of memory.
No wonder Mother hated the idea,
I had to wait until she died to build.
It was her money after all.

                        No,
I never married, never had the time
Or inclination to. Still, getting older,
one wonders...not so much about a wife—
no mystery there—but what about a son.

                  I guess
I always looked for one among my students
and found too many. Never look for what
you truly want. It comes too easily,
and then you never value it enough –

until it's gone—gone like these empty hills
and all the years I spent ignoring them.

There was a boy who lived here years ago—
Named David—a clever handsome boy.
                    He was a student here—
In those rare moments when he chose to study,
But climbing was the only thing he cared for.
It's strange how clearly I remember him.
He lived here off and on almost two years—
In the same room that you are moving into.
You'll like the room. David always did.

Once during a vacation he went off
With friends to climb El Capitan. They took
A girl with them. But it's no easy thing
To climb three thousand feet of granite,
And halfway up, she froze, balanced on a ledge.
They nearly killed themselves to get her down.
At one point David had to wedge himself
Into a crevice, tie down to a rock,
And lower her by rope to another ledge.
When it was over, they were furious.
They drove her back, and he
Surprised me, coming here instead of home.

His clothes were torn, his hands and face cut up.
I went upstairs for bandages, but he
Wanted to shower first. When he called me in,
I watched him standing in the steamy bathroom—
His naked body shining from the water—
Carefully drying himself with a towel.
Then suddenly he threw it down and showed me
Where the ropes had cut into his skin.
It looked as if he had been branded,
Wounds deep enough to hide your fingers in.
I felt like holding him but couldn't bear it.
I helped him into bed and spent the night
Sitting in his room, too upset to sleep.
And on the morning after he drove home.

He graduated just a few months later.
And then went off to Europe where he wrote me
Mainly about beer halls and mountain trips.
I wrote that they would be the death of him.
That spring his mother phoned me when he fell.
I wonder if you know how strange it feels
When someone so much younger than you dies?
And if I tell you something will you not
Repeat it? It is something I don't understand.

The night he died I had a dream. I dreamt
That suddenly the room was filled with light,
Not blinding but the soft whiteness that you see
When heavy snow is falling in the morning,
And I awoke to see him standing there,
Waiting in the doorway, his arms outstretched.
"I've come back to you," he said. "Look at me.
Let me show you what I've done for you."

And only then I saw his skin was bruised,
Torn in places, crossed by deep red welts,
But this time everywhere — as if his veins
Had pushed up to the surface and spilled out.
And there was nothing in his body now,
Nothing but the voice that spoke to me,
And this cold white light pouring through the room.

I stared at him. His skin was bright and pale.
"Why are you doing this to me?" I asked.
"Please, go away."
                          "But I've come back to you.
I'm cold. Just hold me. I'm so very cold."

What else could I have done but hold him there?
I took him in my arms — he was so light —
and held him in the doorway listening.
Nothing else was set or lost it seemed.
We waited there while it grew dark again,
And he grew lighter, slipping silently away
like snow between my fingers, and was gone.

That's all there is to say. I can't explain it,
and now I'm sorry to have bored you so.
It's getting late. You know the way upstairs.
But no, of course not. Let me show you to your room.

HOLY SATURDAY

DEATH DREAMS

arrived at the address, a duplex,
chipped door rocking on its frame.
inside dirt, bare boards,
wind chasing crumpled newspapers.

someone's followed me here, I think.

maybe next door? hey, lights!
people I never much liked
usher me in. a drink? an hors-d'oeuvre?

shadow outside in the bushes.
"who, that? just the guy next door."

* *

at the putt-putt the last hole is death
the one where you don't get your ball back,
I didn't know this. I gaze down the pit
then up at the sky, streaked and lowering.
So this is it. I should've seen the
black flag over the hole, I should've known.
I could've slipped my ball in my pocket,
gone over the back fence.
no one would've noticed me or cared.

* *

we're on an Escher stairwell, some of us
above ground, some below.
who is going up? who coming
down? it just depends on where you
stand. there is another
level, barely seen, high up. footsteps echo
on stone stairs.

* *

In stars: The End.
Underwritten with a flourish.

EASTER

EASTER 1984

When we saw human dignity
healing humans in the middle of the day

we moved in on him slowly
under the incalculable gravity

of old freedom, of our own freedom,
under atmospheres of consequence, of justice

under which no one needs to thank anyone.
If this was God, we would get even.

And in the end we nailed him,
lashed, spittled, stretched him limb from limb.

We would settle with dignity
for the anguish it had caused us,

we'd send it to be abstract again,
we would set it free.

＊

But we had raised up evolution.
It would not stop being human.

Ever afterwards, the accumulation
of freedom would end in this man

whipped, bloodied, getting the treatment.
It would look like man himself getting it.

He was freeing us, painfully, from freedom,
justice, dignity—he was discharging them

of their deadly ambiguous deposit,
remaking out of them the primal day

in which he was free not to have borne it
and we were free not to have done it,

free never to torture man again,
free to believe him risen.

FOR A YOUNG WOMAN
AT EASTER

1

Last night your mother cried.
Your father, comforting her,
could not hold in his anger.
Your brothers and sisters
do not mention your name.

Your son sits in the kitchen,
holding a colored egg.
He will not speak.
Your husband walks like a ghost
through empty rooms.

2

The last time we saw you
you sat at the kitchen table,
untouchable. You said
they'd always taught you
to think of others.
You tossed back your hair:
"Now I'll think of myself."

(IF THESE BUDS)

If these buds, so asleep to my words to my
heart can be held here in my hand with
all the vast struggles and exaltation of my
thoughts being the interval within which
I hold them. . .what tenderness, what
gift they are   held   against this way

why don't we shout out at everything we touch...
The insights of all the history between us
how many suns have exploded, how
many of us have faced our death, how
many of us are watching   here, now
seeing-unseen   in this simple holding

when we touch each other. . .see our children
learning how their bodies weigh in the snow
how high it will exalt them in its drifts
above the hedge, they walk over the hedges
as if walking on waves, or in light
exulting   that we see them

PASCAL AT THE RACES

1

The Gambler: there he is in the old cartoon,
florid and shiny-eyed,
clutched handful of cards.
Other hand in his pocket, groping for
what: an ace, some money,
a gun, a handkerchief
to mop the sweat?

I don't know you, Sir, but you are scary,
with your handful of aces, your possible gun.

The college argumentation competition:
mode: Inspirational.
Back row spectator, my mild speech on reading
not having got itself written, and here comes a Valkyrie
on Gambling. Wild shaggy hair, she pounds the stage.
points and accuses.
Children dying of want, wives gone to the streets.
Visual aids: empty-eyed man in prison
uniform, corpse found in the lake.
Graph falling, red line down and out.
Bingo's almost as bad, it leads to this.

I am in the back. All Catholics gamble.
She gets first prize.
The speech I would have bet on
describes Creative Loafing and doesn't place.

2

wind and horse-stink
here they come:
Charley's Mane, Poker Chip,
Razzmatazz.

I bet on the favorite
always, to show:
pick up $2.20
on my $2 bet.
winning's what counts,
not how much,
no such thing
as a little winner.

3

my granddaughter takes her first step,
the floor rises to strike her,
she's astounded,
the cry collects itself in her throat.

she was betting on air,
thought it was thicker, believed in it,
it would hold her up,
protect her from the violence of the floor.

4

Consider a golden horse on an infinite track,
hooves hitting the line at regular intervals.
You could plot its course,
predict its arrival at point A, point B
to the second. This would be expressible graphically
and no one would bet against you.

Would you bet that 2 + 2
would equal seventy-three?

Here in the text is a picture of the mathematics of chaos,
its coils, brilliant in colors,
the dimensions of chaos,
a chart of the contents of chaos,
a list of the contents of chaos.

5

"Infinite — nothing. Our soul is cast into a body, where it

finds number, time, dimension.
Thereupon it reasons, and calls this nature, necessity, and
    can believe nothing else."

6

smell of beer & peanuts,
sweat & hard luck.

bet every cent on the longshot
& there he is in the last race,
just pulling ahead, out of the crowd,

now a length beyond the others, faster & lighter.
looks like he could fly,
take right off from the track,

headed there now, here now, home.

MY CAMEL, A DIALOGUE
OF SELF AND SOUL

I snared him with a jackknife
and a four-foot length of gut
before his eyes were open,

or they were shut
against me. I cut
his tongue out; I seared

his bloody tongue-root shut.
Sun in your eye,
desert-heart:

do you even know I'm here?
I chew honey-locust pods;
I spit them down his throat.

For years I forget my camel.
He wanders, edged in light,
caked in grit, like a cloud.

Does he wander.
He scents up empty stream beds
with his nostril slits;

he kneels to sleep—
I watch him through the glass.
He's upside down

in the sky; behind
a pyramid, he splits
and crosses the lightest lakes

like Moses. Oh artful,
shaggy, folded:
I write the words

of your name on the lintel,
the gates of my house,
like a cloud,

on my hands' binding,

between my eyes,
so like a cloud.

EASTER VIGIL

The rain is as soft
as a tomb cracking.

With the moon in the West,
around the fire we wait
for the sun.

And against the night
comes the day. Against
the night comes our song
and our brave gathering,
our walking, our circling,
and our standing. We throw
water and fire and smoke
into the night, and
our eating is against the night.

There is the standing up into the air
of all things renewed.
There is the going up into the sky
of the sun.
There are our hearts
being lifted from us toward the day.
Forty days passed at last.
Here now is an end
of waiting.

This is the day that the Lord has made.

MERCY SUNDAY

May 16: St. Brendan

CUSTODY OF THE EYES

Never had it, didn't want it.
I wanted bodies shining, other eyes in mine,
trees, ribbons of dawn, skies without limit,
Every-colored weather and all the faces
Leaping into my skull;
Wanted mazes of canyons, spume of stars
Whatever spiraled flowed, or turning,
changed;
Clouds pouring in, not puffballs
But white fires, roaring, blazing wild
Through the holes in my face, all of them;
Wanted spring earth surging into flesh,
Bark, feathers, skin—trees crazy with cold,
Jagged still with leftover winter
Arms flailing semaphores, twig-fingers
grasping—
Mad for meeting like us all:
like me, like anyone, like God.
I wanted a seraph's ravished heart,
Not believing I'd become all eyes
Unless I let my own go their way,
Unless I gave my eyes custody of me.

So I let the sun, frozen coin, hurricane of light,
Beat at all my gaping eyes
Even as I learned to be a priest.
Most of my brothers walked softly
Heads bowed, trusting a gift of rest
That felt to me a stone's calculus.
Even if I thought of learning stillness—
Scrubbing plank floors white
Feeling wheat fall shining, live
Nailing the world's kaleidoscope
To Jesus's heart as you walked or worked,
Letting your clumsy jumble stop
A light on still water, clear

A circle of self's repose —
I said (if anyone asked), "Let me see!
Let it come in, let me go out."

Each evening we walked alone, together;
The beads chimed in my fingers too,
Slow in the quiet fading light —
The mysteries blooming in the autumn
          leaves,

Huddling naked through Lenten Marches
Dazzling the lobes of my May soaked
          brain —
As my eyes stalked hawks and planets,
Snatched at the bread of miracles that
          churned
By the thousand down the slopes of blue
That rose from twilight earth to heaven.
I said them, yes, believed them
Even when my chainless eyes
Came home empty, beggared, begging,
Drooling like idiots of grief,
And asked for everything, all of me.
They promised-not even mercy.

None. They hauled me out in midsleep
To nights like eternal years
To streets where April snow hushed and squeezed
The city to a line of pale desert,
Demanded morning for me past the stars.
Had I let my black shoes balance them
With care along the required way
God might have sooner let me see
Darkness whole, peace in my heart's
          wreckage.

But how could l recalculate,
My mind sucked out through the windows
Flung up the funnel's violence

With scrapbooks, photos, friendly rooms
      and voices
All my resting-places strewn galaxies-wide,
My yielded will hammered fine
A wire forged to pull me in
By yanking me wholly out?

Lord, I wanted the holes in my face
Open—the only way I trusted—
To the wild furnace of the sun,
To a world eaten by its own fire,
To eyes famished for wonder like mine;
But I never guessed the charred sockets,
Ears and nose burned to the bone,
Mouth blasted, endless blackened shout,
All my blood a plasma of emptiness.
I am going up in smoke.
The insatiable fuses of my eyes
Powdering my heart faster than light
Draw me bone by sinew, cell by synapse
Into the final holocaust of silence.
Eyeless, wordless, faceless I have gone.
Jesus: I begin.

SYNCRETISM

We transubstantiated our own Eucharist
Today; I was sitting in the front row.
Mackintosh apples and cider
Became the Body and Blood of Christ,
Served on the golden platen
Of an IBM compatible portable.
Angels flew up on pulleys into the ceiling —
Stage scenery was
Down as banners.
Father presided happily costumed in
Liturgical green as
Altar boys skittered
Like stage hands wearing
Frocks smocks tennis shoes and Budweiser
T-shirts underneath.
Water.
Sister blessed us with water.
We took an oath falling from hi-tech
Speakers heard on high.
The promises were gender neutral —
Mary the Goddess as well as God.
"It was an invention learned in college,"
Priest said, jolly gut like Santa Claus,
"Appropriate for these occasions."
I had to chew and crunch hard on the
Red-skinned Body of
Christ,
Saying on stage
In front of the assembly:
"This is my Body,
Amen."
The play had a Byzantine plot. A kneeling
Atheist professor looked on in
Awe at the majesty of the
Almighty —
Time past,
Present
One —
God.

QUID PRO QUO

Just after my wife's miscarriage (her second
in four months), I was sitting in an empty
classroom exchanging notes with my friend,
a budding Joyce scholar with steelrimmed
glasses, when, lapsed Irish Catholic that he was,
he surprised me by asking what I thought now
of God's ways toward man. It was spring,

such spring as came to the flintbacked Chenango
Valley thirty years ago, the full force of Siberia
behind each blast of wind. Once more my poor wife
was in the local four-room hospital, recovering.
The sun was going down, the room's pinewood panels
all but swallowing the gelid light, when, suddenly,
I surprised not only myself but my colleague

by raising my middle finger up to heaven, *quid
pro quo*, the hardly grand defiant gesture a variant
on Varmi Fucci's figs, shocking not only my friend
but in truth the gesture's perpetrator too. I was 24,
and, in spite of having pored over the *Confessions*
& that Catholic Tractate called the *Summa*, was sure
I'd seen enough of God's erstwhile ways toward man.

That summer, under a pulsing midnight sky
shimmering with Van Gogh stars, in a creaking,
cedarscented cabin off Lake George, having lied
to the gentrified owner of the boys' camp
that indeed I knew wilderness & lakes and could,
if need be, lead a whole fleet of canoes down
the turbulent whitewater passages of the Fulton Chain

(I who had last been in a rowboat with my parents
at the age of six), my wife and I made love, trying
not to disturb whosever headboard & waterglass
lie just beyond the paperthin partition at our feet.

In the great black Adirondack stillness, as we lay
there on our sagging mattress, my wife & I gazed out
through the broken roof into a sky that seemed

somehow to look back down on us, and in that place,
that holy place, she must have conceived again,
for nine months later in a New York hospital she
brought forth a son, a little buddha-bellied
rumplestiltskin runt of a man who burned
to face the sun, the fact of his being there
both terrifying & lifting me at once, this son,

this gift, whom I still look upon with joy & awe.
        Worst,
best, just last year, this same son, grown
to manhood now, knelt before a marble altar to vow
everything he had to the same God I had had my own
erstwhile dealings with. How does one bargain
with a God like this, who, *quid pro quo*, ups
the ante each time He answers one sign with another?

THE HOUSE

The table, son, is laid
with the quiet whiteness of cream,
and on four walls ceramics
gleam blue, glint light.
Here is the salt, here the oil,
in the center, bread that almost speaks.
Gold more lovely than gold of bread
is not in broom plant or fruit,
and its scent of wheat and oven
gives unfailing joy.
We break bread, little son, together
with our hard fingers, our soft palms,
while you stare in astonishment
that black earth brings forth a white flower.

Lower your hand that reaches for food
as your mother also lowers hers.
Wheat, my son, is of air,
of sunlight and hoe;
but this bread, called "the face of God,"
is not set on every table.
And if other children do not have it,
better, my son, that you not touch it,
better that you do not take it
with ashamed hands.

My son, Hunger with his grimaced face
in eddies circles the unthrashed wheat.
They search and never find each other,
Bread and hunchbacked Hunger.
So that he find it if he should enter now,
we'll leave the bread until tomorrow.
Let the blazing fire mark the door

that the Quechuan Indian never closed,
and we will watch Hunger eat
to sleep with body and soul.

translated by Doris Dana

*In Chile, the people call bread "The face of God." (G. M.)

May 16: St. Brendan

ST. BRENDAN'S PRAYER

Looking West from Dun Chaoin
Over the Blasket Islands

Sky sky sky is the word,
Just one shout in the direction
Of the blue vastness which weighs
Nothing and everything,

No one word can convey
How sky stings, pierces and turns
Inside out the heart of a man,
Scourges him delirious with the question
He is but cannot frame, because
Sky frames all questions, always
Stretching the asked and the asker
To the limitless blue
Upon blue upon blue deeps,

Questioning, which is fire,
Spangling night in glinting shoals
Of sidereal time, till the mind
Reels, besotted with splendour,
Questioning, which ignites the body,
Burns up every leaf of the mind,
Consumes the mind's roots, the heart,
In the smelter of spirit, till the soul
Pools, gleaming, breathing red gold,

Sky all world, sky lights up,
Kindles with the coming sun,
Throws everything into unbearable relief,
We twist, maddened by the light
Of dawn, closing its disclosing
With departure, we stumble away,
Ever looking backwards to behold
The staggering Beauty for which
We were born belonging,
Any shadow will do,

Where we hope not to die of regret,
Because we forget just enough
To remember only sorrow, or better yet,
To feel nothing at all,
Than surrender to sky, star sky,
Grevious sky of radiant daybreak.

Is there one, is there anywhere
One who will bend sky down, rend
Its awful vastness and descend,
The day reined in within His ardent
Glance, His wounds the burning stars
Which cover me with constellations
Of compassion, and be, Himself
My firmament and friend?

BRIEF SONG OF THE BEACH SAND

How blessed at sundown, lying serene
Along the sloping beach in burnished
Fans of gold, you sea-wet sand,

In the Making, you were rushing red rivers
Of stone molten, then slowly cooling,
Hid in aeons of shut grey, where counting
Is defeated, bewildered and awed,

The Sacred Rain, wielding Its soul as sky-fire,
Struck the peak, where, as continents
Tilted and thrust, groaning, you had arisen,
Sheared the pinnacle beyond you in blinding
Blasts of scorching white light, cleaving
Away debris, till, suddenly, you gazed free,
From the height, wordless, sight sheer joy,

Sun the First gazed on you in his ardent
Daybreak, you gulped down the liquor of his heat
Upon the thirsty mountaintops, until
In His Bright Beauty, enkindled again and again,
You broke, startled for long just a widening fissure
Of pain, slowly slipping, then suddenly
Sliding loose, shattering, exploding
In fragments flung out from the sharp
Fells of the mountainside, to a shifting
Tumble of scree, restless until snows held you
Stilled, silenced in their terrible embrace,
Slowly pulverizing, moraine dragging
Downslope, till thaws loosened grit
Into the bounding freshets of spring,

Holy Wind, God's Breath, ever seeking
In Its strong passion, lifted you, threw you up
Free into the rushing bright air, carried high
Over mountains in roiling updraughts,
To be, in settling breezes, broadcast across

Restless waving green grass seas of the prairies,
Or billowed softly down into the solemn dance
Of the desert's pure white dunes, none
Here seeing you save Eagle soaring high,

Till, passing through rapids and sloughs in the dark
Hidden river of time, not ours, but earth's
And the stars' and the ageless air's time,
The rain-brooms swept you into a spate
Roistering into the River to the Sea, where,
In late afternoon, shooting the bucking, standing
Waves of the watersmeet, you were thrown
Deep into the white mercy cascading
As jade-blue breakers topple and fall, there
Cleansed and gravely winnowed, now wavelet
On wavelet have bathed you to rest, laying you
Upon the dun grey shores of middle earth,
Appalled upon the world's edge,

Here, for an hour, a week, or a season,
The blue white waves lend you their voice,
Here you behold the three realms at once,
The land, the sky and sea, and feel
The breath of the unseen fourth,

Here in borrowed words you seethe and sigh
Your memories of epochs fallen out of ken,
Here, to the measure of waves, you croon,
Humming beneath melody, brief songs of all
That ends so it may at last begin,

You so silently chant with shore reeds
For a pipe, with the skirl of gannets, the screech
Of gulls, ritornellos of the sanderlings,
And, for a drum, the nearly silent thrum
Of an unwalked beach seeming taut
From the tide's last lingering caress,

Till you glisten, rich in silence,
Anointed for the liturgy of sundown,
Being now only the compassion of rock,
Ground by a mercy and pain and a desire
All unspeakable, to sand, holy strand,
Awash, awake, all ache of all things being,

After a time and a time and half a time,
The strong, gentle arms of the neap
Tide lift you from your bed, and,
Tenderest of hands, draw you down,
Enthralled, into the sapphire halls of the sea,
Now chartless in the world-wide waters'
Sway, dancing their elegant pavane
With sun and moon and wind, as the stars
So softly ring the changes of the heavens
In everlasting measures of sidereal time,

Here the light pours down in crystal shafts,
Flickering blue green-gold from sky-light above,
As you drift, sparkling at last, to rest awhile
In the still, silent riffles of the rocky shelf,

Old as earth, ingrained with high knowledge
And with low, come through many deaths
Of love, hid here dimly radiant beneath
The wings of the One Who broods
The world from its Making
To its Arising New.

In Honor of Saint Brendan the Navigator
Dedicated to Paul Christensen, Sailor, Oblate, Friend
September 14 to October 6, 1996
Carmel, Rincon, Valyermo

ASCENSION OF OUR LORD

May 30: St. Joan Of Arc

ASCENSION

Stretching Himself as if again,
      through downpress of dust
                  upward, soil giving way
to thread of white, that reaches
      for daylight, to open as green
              leaf that it is...
Can Ascension
      not have been
              arduous, almost,
as the return
      from Sheol, and
              back through the tomb
into breath?
      Matter reanimate
              now must relinquish
itself, its
      human cells,
              molecules, five
senses, linear
      vision endured
              as Man —
the sole
      all-encompassing gaze
              resumed now,
Eye of Eternity.
      Relinquished, earth's
              broken Eden.
Expulsion,
      liberation,
              last
self-enjoined task
      of Incarnation.
              He again
Fathering Himself
      Seed-case
              splitting,
He again
      Mothering His birth:
              torture and bliss.

CHRIST BRINGS LIGHT
TO THE PROVINCES

Light was all the rage that year
and when he claimed it
the populace fell round itself
concentrically in swoons
and offered him their loyalty,
their sons, their feisty goats.
Tired of stubbing their toes,
of groping for doorknobs in the dark,
they called on him to end them,
imagining the afterlife as advertised.

He only stood there, fragile
as a seahorse tooth, holding
their dogged love like a bag
filled with broken glass.
Then he walked right past them
till he came to the forest
of a nation without eyes or windows.
There, rising up on just one inhalation,
he smiled down benignly on the trees,
then burst the air sharply
like a ruptured hive of livid bees,
shedding ashes and scales
in a blizzard of redress.

BALANCE AND LEVER

You're perched on the shed roof's unstable edge
bending to secure the ragged fascia broken by a storm, as if
a promontory battered all day with sliding foam and in-sucked eddies,
blown spume, pounding combers like a heavy heartbeat below a base
          of rocks;
but this burnished point is two-dimensional and silent. You've noticed
how young the wind can seem, swirling scent of straw and wire,
and the taste of nails. But so intent on a blush of chalk-line
against the weathered lumber you miss the signs: the leaf-light unreels,
a steeplechase of clouds intercepts the sun; at last the clearing hardly-
          blue
makes you look high past the feathered tip of eucalyptus. Turning,
          paired,
the hawks bank and rise like bits of ash, but sentient, seeing you
with some ultimate acuity clinging to your hopeful raft
that seems so rudderless on the grassy waves. There are no phrasing
          indicators
in this manuscript, which consists almost entirely of the subject's
repetition, unfolding, marked by impersonal notes of grandeur
and despair. So much would seem to need translation
but you are in a trembling vaulted place figured with hawks and
          contrails
remembering the passion of a childhood and the string and winds
that lifted you on the choral texture, from *Come Ye Daughters*,
to the *Alas My Jesus Now Is Taken*, breathless and afraid. It's not your
          fault:
hawks and light drew the bitterness from your mouth. You didn't
will this grace that nails you like a shingle to your felt and metal
balcony, out of plumb and apt to broil you in another reckless hour.
The pasture seems to heave and sail you home. You've laid
your chores aside and heard the instrumental sarabande conclude
this deepest grief watches at the tomb of everyone.

COMING UP

1

The sirens sound this close, this urgent now
the 2nd week of May,
    a movement of air reordering stakes,
cadenzas trimmed with arbor bees
    and cardinals. The wind out of Saskatchewan
might make some sense of it,
    bringing a turn on season's change, and the days
ahead of him, like so much stone to cut,
    leaving the tower fenced, the park-house down,
where she, lavender half-slip, bra,
    had listened and explained, where after-imaging
took hold, within the play of a day's spices.
    He breathes their sufferable dust, breathes deep
the notes a kid might copy out of air, above
    the desk-top miniatures, listening to the sirens speak,
the E.M.S., Police, the whine of the house cat
    sprawled on cellar stone or kitchen hardwood.
And thinks the sirens speak to him, saying
    what calls he must return, before the coins run out,
before the family finds its last erasures
    in his lifetime. Whatever the words would come of it,
her lingering haunts him yet, and afterthoughts,
    like cheap desiderata, whatever it was that drove him then,
    between the Bismarck and the highschool,
to launch the colored glass he might have turned in
    for deposit, to hear, in glass and school-brick,
the sounds arise to spare him his skewed faith,
    releasing him from the nuns' glide,
from meals they led boys to, after how many sad feasts...
    The stars fit well enough, leaving a boy
to all his dread of mispossession, the squinting kid
    still posed, at stake if he could find a way
to tell the camera, searching signs in the made tales
    their dying left to him. The stars
fit well enough, and nights speed-reading inks

test-proven for impermanence, the cemetery spooks,
lusting after him, tucked now behind
      the mystery of numbers, in the rise and set of years,
the rush of seasons as one kiss, in the stories
      stored, under the lids screwed down, and in the wood
heard scream, threatening to split.

2

1965, when the ballplayers played through all the vanishing

He muddles poem by poem. Curbstones
shatter and seem glass. Lost in another childhood,
he stands up in that hot bath, bearing as sunlight bore
each new conception of a planet, excited by lyrics,
fresh loaves, by mothers offering their lives, altering
arcs for boys with what was left them after budgets...
God, he thinks, who might be moved by their thanksgivings,
marvels over us. And we, cutting boasts
into park wood, we make our nights of it, whooping
the ashes up, feeling the words form stiffly
and the season burn them in, there, at the start of holiday,
the season subtracting boys, and the boys,
descending park steps into ballfields, come with enough to play,
friends there, at the ends of schooling,
and the friends gone off, like stones, well-pleased
for having found out stones could walk...
So Revelation sits on us, and frets of storm, and noise-making
turned the chief of many interests, laying-in
fresh tracks. And the voices, fracturing long blocks,
blue, and bringing memorabilia to bear, ask
the boys again to hurry when the relatives come by,
making a sound like cloudwork then, and sounds
like water funneling, of boys, and fathers, looking
after boys, their voices like snot gears, grinding
one half-decade down to proverbs.

3

He pulls his stuck shirt free, resisting mirrors,
feeling the form and sweep,

the crescendos and feathery lines that seemed pre-flesh
diamonding for him, Beauty again
distracting him from family, and that boy
suffering Beauty's forms,
finding the lay of first idea in her advent flesh.
So many real lives, mis-read as consummations,
having come to their news' worth,
in play and suspended play, scared to taverns and to beds,
waking scared to lift their first juice glass
of the day's congress. Hadn't the riptide Latin almost
worked on him, come to his full height, taking
the speakers at their word, dropping from league play
to compositions under street-lamps?

As panicky and lost as he believes himself to be,
he sees himself full length, bothering solved locks,
entering rooms arranged in obligato waves, the notes
repeating without shade, *dresser, bed,*
and free-standing closet, finding the absorbed
first-hand accounts, a child studying his piano
in a studied house, expecting the world from these,
come home with latitudes to bear, and from
the boys that wait for him, fierce
in their own thinking.

4

He searches the drizzle of first words, struck
by the logic, stroke by stroke, by the language
honed to pass along a bargain, and now by galaxies
set spin, by fists like a percussion dropping off
from the raw matter. Could he believe the half of it,
discovering his preference for bass, for dusk
and dusk's pursuits, tall among these lives, and on
that grid of lives, in wave-play and ellipses,
believe the obliterate advance, the lives cleared out,
like merchandise, like parts of speech, alight
in their discretion over prices?
The soup-kitchen, flower-bearing dead
will leave the child another round at instruments.
And these last hues now, along the tree-lawn edge

of Simon, will set her image there, tilt her face
that asks with whom shall he stand by, that suffers
and waits the indecision in his gazing. He sees
too little to see, gone now from air as at the turn
of a new stairwell, into the notes another time,
into the chill he dresses for, into the words, he thinks,
like first conditionings, and Love that seems
to lack a speaker after all.

May 30: St. Joan Of Arc

THE VISIONS AND VOICES
OF JEANNE D'ARC

Dedicated to Father Arthur Young
Friar Minor Conventual

I

I woke up in a robin's nest, I heard Him say "Rise little girl." But what could I say when I rose that morning? — that someone had come to comfort the disquieted, to disquiet the comfortable. The Rose of Sharon is purple and green, after The Fall comes The Spring... resurexit sicut dixut, alleluia, alleluia, the gentle descent of clouds, this morning the sky is dyed lavender as an Easter egg. I was like Thomas (the doubting twin) but I suspended my disbelief. Belief held by surface tension as a needle floats in a bath. I saw a cave and a stone directed against it. I am the leaf that trembles against the glass. Can you hear voices in the leaves?

II

1. I will believe till the stain glass breaks and Jesu Christe, my lover is a priest feeding the eucharist to birds. 2. Then I will press his kisses between bible pages and grow old. 3. I will never live longer. 4. The devil mocks me, says my vision, my voices are fraud, my country a prostitute. 5. He has put a pit in my mouth. 6. There is one drop of doubt in the stone. 7. But last night in the spring snow storm there was lightning, the sky split apart and I saw The Holy Family. Jesu, Marie, Joseph. 8. When the Bishop of France blessed me I did not bow my head. I have always kissed with my eyes open. He held my face with his hands each side like a dove's wings.

III

As before the battle, in God's name I will not retreat. Tonight the sky is banked and heaped with little stars on the rim of a dying universe. (Did my God say "veni, vedi, veci"? Or "I came. I saw. I left"?) I don't remember most of my life. I look into the mirror they have given me to dress as a maiden but do not see myself. From my cell one sparrow lies beside his widow, repeats and repeats ("je-sus, je-sus, je-sus"). Oh, Christ, when will you come? I hear many birds say as they fly away... "I'm sorry, I'm sorry, I'm sorry."

ON FIRE

It begins as combustion, this making of heat
and light —

She is last seen in a field, on fire.
Flames tongue her cuffs, lick both sleeves,
unbutton her collar. She runs clothed
in red firelight. Her hair vanishes into ash,
her body drops like a charred doll.

Meanwhile, a monk on the other side
of the world falls beneath a spinning fan.
What force pulls this whirl of wind and
fire downward? Smoke rises, leaving behind
a holy relic. He foresaw this as a blessed
passing, death by fire in the sign of Aries.

One instant the illusion of a solid body,
the next, candle ends and kindling.
The remnants of a life rise up, sunlight
descending into trees.

PENTECOST

PSALM #5

Like a deer or its hunter,
You watch for me each morning
in the twigs,
in the whole earth
which rises through wetness,
sleep.

I ready myself,
in the discipline of a supplicant.

Hear me.

Your favor covers the virtuous man.

Let me walk upright,
clad in the sun, high days,
my spear in hand.
Let a riot of flowers
attend me, little soldiers, strong-stemmed,
with their laughter, their
opened, now-here,
now-there faces.

THE EMERALD DOVE

We ought to hang cutout hawk shapes
in our windows. Birds hard driven
by a predator, or maddened by a mirrored rival
too often die zonk against the panes'
invisible sheer, or stagger away from
the blind full stop in the air.
It was different with the emerald dove.
In at an open sash, a pair

sheered, missile, in a punch of energy,
one jinking on through farther doors, one
thrown, panicked by that rectangular wrong copse, braked
like a bullet in blood, a full-on splat of wings
like a vaulter between shoulders, blazed and calliper,
ashriek out of jagbeaked fixed fury, swatting wind,
lights, keepsakes, panes, then at the in window out, gone.
A sparrowhawk, by the cirrus feathering.

The other, tracked down in a farther room
clinging to a bedhead, was the emerald dove,
a rainforest bird, flashed in beyond its world
of lice, sudden death and tree seeds. Pigeon-like,
only its eye and neck in liquid motion,
there as much beyond us as beyond
itself, it perched, barefoot in silks
like a prince of Sukhothai, above the reading lamps and cotton-buds.

Modest-sized as a writing hand, mushroom fawn
apart from its paua casque, those viridescent closed wings,
it was an emerald Levite in that bedroom
which the memory of it was going to bless for years
despite topping our ordinary happiness, as beauty
makes background of all around it. Levite too
in the question it posed: sanctuary without transformation,
which is, how we might be,

plunged out of our contentment into evolved strange heaven,

where the need to own or mate with or eat the beautiful
was bygone as poverty,
and we were incomprehensibly, in our exhaustion,
treasured, cooed at, then softly left alone
among vast crumples, verticals, refracting air,
our way home barred by mirrors, our splendour unmanifest
to us now, a small wild person, with no idea of peace.

THE LANGUAGE OF ANGELS

One hundred geese—no, more
than a hundred—came down from the sky
and landed in the golden field

south of my house. At first I was startled
by the great commotion until I remembered
when that flock of geese first appeared

and wedged itself into the topography
of my brain. Or maybe
I hadn't forgotten, just pulled the memory

out toward the mouth of a cave,
autumn leaping and turning
cottonwood leaves to flame, faith

still coming down from the sky in tongues
to anoint the genes with a memory
so that we might evolve toward the shape of

say, an angel—part bird, part human—
on the inside, in the quiet of our minds,
as if opening a book

to see the scramble of words on the page
like a flock of geese rise
and somehow find its pleasing shape.

GOD COMPARES THE SOUL
TO FOUR THINGS
—*after Mechthild of Magdeburg*

Aged in the cask of bodily stillness —
　　　　　O delectable wine!

Risen from the censer of bodily devotion —
　　　　　O fragrant incense!

Filled with the fire of bodily purity —
　　　　　O refulgent gem!

Rung from the bell of bodily abandon,
　　　　　O thrilling sound!

CORPUS CHRISTI

August 11: St. Clare

DESIGN

My mother tells me how this morning
the man who plays piano at the church
brought my father communion after mass,
so I ask if she had him break the Host
in half, had told him she did not go,
say he could do that, she agreeing
but saying she never thought to ask,
which I think is so my martyr mother,
but do not say, turning instead to how
a light snowfall made walking difficult,
how I had thought of her, wondered if
she had gone, was glad that she had not,
remembering how I had brought my father
communion at the hospital Christmas Eve,
how frail he had looked as he opened up
his hands to receive the Host,
as if he were letting free the flutter of a moth.
"Mother," I said, remembering her alone
at the window, "take care of yourself.
He is letting go. You and I must trust
design to govern in all things. Within
this house a moth through winter lives."

RELIGIOUS AUTOBIOGRAPHY

Head bowed, kneeling to pray in the pew,
you cough the host out from under
your tongue, the coined body of Christ,

unleavened and legended. You know
you can't equivocate this blunder —
the nun-spun tales even atheists

fear bounce in your mind like bees
off leaded-glass panes. The stolen host,
the dagger. Unstoppable blood. Scenes

of sinners on their knees and the priest
in his robe conversing with God, the ghost
of a hand removing the screen,

the moon-like face in the half-lit room
of apology, the man who was haunted
in dreams by red-running rivers and stones

shedding tears by a radiant tomb.
You lower your head, holding the bread
on your tongue, abruptly alone

in the church with the crucified Christ —
hole in his side, shadows below,
heaven and earth, hand and the heart:

Swallow it man, lest the rest fall apart.

ADORATION AT 2 A.M.

Only a layman, you have your practiced
Ritual nonetheless. Wife and daughters
Asleep, you try to nap, or channel-surf
For innocent reruns, then shower, shave,
Dress, read something (perhaps) appropriate,
And drive into the early morning night.

You follow these streets in every season:
Through lightning and blown rain in troubled spring,
Or humid blackness of still midsummer;
Under drifting moons in sudden autumn,
Or clear, far stars that make the winter sky.
The trip itself is a step out of time.

At journey's end, a stranger like you will
Surrender his vigil. You take his place
Before the monstrance filled with what we seek
And repray old promises for an hour.

Back home again, you dream briefly toward dawn.

August 11: St. Clare

ST. CLARE—SUMMER NIGHT, SCATTERED CLOUDS

A full moon plays with the clouds
above Clare's Basilica.
It slips behind the waves and
reappears, unnoticed where
bright floodlights hold her docked tomb
still beneath the lolling clouds.
I can almost hear patter
as water drips from the moon
rowing from her church's prow.

CLARE, THE SAINT

Since a child I have been drawn
to the Sun, the pleasure it gleans

from Its senseless abandonment, Its furious mane
like a caravan camped in the desert, born

from the betrayal of body, each dawn
into eternity. What I have seen

and endured, I will imitate, wean
myself off of this world, be done

with sensation, the smoke from smoldering husks
rearing up sickly sweet with its promise

of flame and in turn dismember
my wardrobe, stack up this hair as if brush,

bend my bones as if kindling, so the Sun's kiss
reduces my resistance into embers.

ASSUMPTION

August 23: St. Rose of Lima

SNOW IN THE WOODS

I

The child Christ of Prague
held out his toy globe
to the dirt road past the window

and the Popes shined down
from frames to the Madonnas,
ceramic, and full of love.

The holy water stood with the spices.

II

Only snow in the woods, the aunts would say
when the grandfather wandered back
drunk as spring,

when the uncles sickened and died
from coal dust settling
to dark drifts in their lungs.

My first love: St. Jude.

My first dance was croup in a waterless house.

III

Snow took its time like a disability check
while my aunts held their breath
and blessed themselves,

and then blessed me —
the little cluster of pomegranate,

the little plot wanting seed —
saying the old prayer
to the virgin on the sill:

Let her learn to close her hands
and be covered;

let her go into the dark
to say her sins;

let her come out cool and bright
as the pine limb or the stone

or the winter hive frosted.
Promise her sweet in the sun.

August 23: St. Rose of Lima

CHURCH OF ROSE OF LIMA, CINCINNATI

it looks from the hill like something
fra angelico painted, the red
rectangular lines and the bricked bell
steepled out of time. this church
honors saint rose in a city
as spare of peruvians as miracles.

it floods out whenever the river rises
and has a smell of common water
at the altars, and pilots of tows
on long hauls from pennsylvania
needle the dark with searching lights
to catch the hour off her clock.

saint rose keeps a timid time.
I've heard her bell strike three
as if an afternoon surprised her.
the church itself may well surprise her.
in lima she has golden altars; germans
made them wood on the unliturgical river.

but churches anywhere seem rude for her.
this virgin kept a hidden time
and the world could give no wedding ring
to wed her with. her lover came quick
and killed the peruvian roses she grew fond
and the small buds withered in the winter fog

once I thought the rococo christ
had made her a violent dove and held
her trembling in his hand like a bell.
I am not so sure of this today.
she may be undiscoverable, like silt
slow rivers encourage into islands.

ST. ROSE OF LIMA
(Rose died in 1617 at age 31)

> *How well I know the spring,*
> *Gushing and flowing,*
>   *Though it be dark.*
> —St. John of the Cross

I am the smelly rat that bolts swill and scurries
Windlike. The rat is pure. Her match? The crown of spikes
That spurs the skittish novice to discipline.
I'm not the silk-donned marquise, noisy and gay, who likes
To nibble sweetmeats and flirt stealthily, who worries

If a prissy don stares at a pimple on her nose.
Vanity is wine to gentlefolk, ratsbane to me.
Though nature-bestowed, a pretty face and dainty hands
Scar the virgin soul; clever repartee only shows
A lack of fortitude. Heaven exacts a simple fee —

Agony. Well-thumbed rosaries or dog-eared missals
Won't suffice; the dowry must be of flesh and blood.
Is this heresy? Faith is like a moth, delicate and bright,
That flits and dallies in the night She's Satan's food.
He lurks in my heart, his net woven from the bristles

Of his crackly hide. I feel bloated as with child
This demon's drool burns my bosom raw; within flares
A host of wild roses. The vile runt screaks and rattles
My rib cage crossed; I hear the trill of wedding bells, mild
And ravishing. Saint Catherine agrees caution impairs

One's faculties. Through foul seas one must sail a caravel,
Not a galleon. On tortuous roads a steed is steadier
Than a jade. Beware, these ways are choked. At every turn
Weedy nuns are crawling on their veils. On foggy days a
       ladder
Drops and sways, beckoning. Once I held on fast but fell

Into a smoky privy pit, boundless. Above, a storm raged, a dark and
        whirring cloud of birds. A vulture swept
Upon my blackened face and plucked my giddy eyes. I laughed.
Penance is sweet in dreadful dreams. My bed is light and warm,
A manger of thorns and broken glass. Plain Mary wept

At bloody Calvary; I sleep in joyful Bethlehem.
These pricks and shards are cupid's aids. So too are the chemise
I sewed from mares' manes and the cutting chain belt I wear.
Am I Eve? To woo our Lord takes daring. Though shabby, he's
Fickle as racking clouds, but I'm bold as desert rain. A hymn

Or prayer is not a rapier drawn or a crossbow strained,
But anchors cast in choppy coves or corn sowed in salty earth.
Our lives are like onion skin adrift in a gale
That rips the lofty sail. How is hope then sustained?
Like a bee I sew and pray tirelessly. An hour's labor is worth

A holiday in Galilee, where alabaster hills are gilt
With hermits' caves, ewe's milk rivulets revive the fallow field,
And honey dew speckles fodder, grove, meadow. Such a happy land.
The lamb bounds into her shepherd's arms; ancient wells yield
Fragrant wine at dusk. In our shady garden my father built

A hut of splintered stones and mucky straw. This is my cave,
Sinner's bower and carapace. In vernal nights, crickets girth my home,
Chirping twinkly serenades. Strays wail a dirge or two.
Heads or tails, the doubloon still falls; hide-and-seek, the knave
Is caught easily. The sloughs dry, I gallop sidesaddle to starry Rome.

ORDINARY TIME

October 1: St. Therese

October 4: St. Francis

October 18: St. Luke
(Patron Saint of Painters)

October 31: All Souls

November 1: All Saints

AUGUST PRAYER

The monks chant their prayer in the hot church
but their heart is not in it.
Only their vows bring them and keep them
at the hot and useless task.

Gone are the sweet first good days
when prayer and singing came easy
Gone as well many brothers
who used to stand here singing
        the feasts with them.

They know there are ways to beat this heat
and that Americans everywhere are finding them;
but they beat instead the tones of psalms
and, *by beating,*
        fall through the layers of heat
        and the layers of prayer

        and are standing there now
        only with their sound
        and their sweat

everything taken from them
except the way that this day in August has been.

DAILY BREAD

A gull far-off
rises and falls, are of a breath,
two sparrows pause on the telephone wire,
chirp a brief interchange, fly back to the ground,
the bus picks up one passenger and zooms on up the hill,
across the water the four poplars
conceal their tremor, feet together, arms pressed to their
            sides,
behind them the banked conifers dark and steep;
my peartree drops a brown pear from its inaccessible height
into the bramble and ivy tangle, grey sky
whitens a little, now one can see vague forms of cloud
pencilled lightly across it.
This is the day that the Lord hath made,
let us rejoice and be glad in it.

BUTTERFLIES
(Nicaragua, December 1996)

They are like
Snow, in the
Full bodied light.
Swirling, misting
The road.

Children stand
And let the
Dusty millions
Wing them,
Trip along them,
Tickle them, like
A fumbling lover.

And I
Pity them
When crushed
Under tires,
Love them
For this
Obsessive desire —
To cross the road.

CORRIDORS

Neither reminiscent of the sun's light
through a maple leaf nor of dense green
lawns on dew mornings, the corridors that
veined St. Mary's Elementary were unlike

any green a god would have a hand in.
Pale, dusty, cobwebbed, cracked
and mottled with decades' worth
of children's fingerprints, the walls

rejected sound and soul. The merest
whisper bounded through the halls like wind,
and nuns at their most cat-like still clacked
heels on linoleum so hard our knees bruised

when we genuflected. Certainly our prayers
could rise no higher than the ceiling
where they lingered, possibly forever,
like accumulating layers of smoke.

This explained why God seemed not to hear them.
During class, only spiders crawled the hallway.
Coats and caps hung shapelessly from pegs
and waited, imitations of our souls

someday in purgatory. Either Catholic time
was longer than time paced by measures other
than eternity, or the sister turned the clock
back while we sang, eyes shut in terror

or in devotion to a Father who would blast
us down to hell if He didn't love us
for occasional perfections, our voices
straining faintly through tight shingles.

CONSECRATION

Come! I will show you the bride....
          —Apocalypse 21:9

It was at home: Mama was cooking,
I was taking care of the baby.
Restless, because of the boy who was waiting for me.
The baby's wet, I called,
I'm going to change him.
Mama shot me a look and I went to my room
and tried on dresses to wear to the door
and talk with the boy who whispered:
I want to eat your legs, your belly, your breasts,
I want to touch you.
And he was in fact touching me, the way his soul
shone through his eyes.
Have you changed the baby?
You're a strange one!
Stop talking to your friends and listen!
I began to cry: pleasure and embarrassment.
He looked at my bare feet and laughed.
The vibrations of the flesh sing hymns,
even those we turn away from:
flatulence (he said in one ear)
yawns (he said in the other)
the rhythm of pleasure.
—I was worried the whole time.
—And so naive and naked, he added,
a voluptuous woman in her bed
can praise God,
even if she is nothing but voluptuous and happy.
—Poor people understand that. . .
—Yes, like when they write on the walls:
US BEGGARS SALUTE YOU, O GOD!
He looked like an angel, speaking of wisdom. . .
Helios, I called him, you're that luminescent,
your body acting out your spirit.

—You learn fast, praise be Our Lord Jesus Christ,
he intoned from the bottom of his Christian soul,
enticing me once and for all.
Who is the pope? I asked, anxious to receive the sacraments.
—Our Father Who blesses us.
And he called me cow, as if he were saying flower, saint,
lucky prostitute.

BREAKFAST DISHES

Her children at her constantly, she feels
like the scarecrow in *The Wizard of Oz*:
out of nowhere a son flies by and steals
a beak of straw so fast she cannot pause
to think for just one second if she ate
her breakfast yet. The morning's been a blur.
And now her oldest daughter tells her straight
she'd rather not be seen in church with her.
Where are those nuns, she wonders, who instilled
in her throughout her college years that mothering
a flock like hers would make her feel fulfilled
in God. How dare her daughter call her smothering.
She imagines sisters back from morning prayers,
ending their fast with tea and cream eclairs.

LOVE GAME

I'm hopelessly in love with a girl called Life;
she sends me messages smudged with her tears,
proposes rendezvous but rarely keeps them,
rings me at midnight (agitating stars),
but has, she says, another call on the line,
and rings back later when I'm not at home,
tells me she loves me but when I respond
turns her head away or pleads a cold,
wears frowsy gear and looks for compliments,
and dresses elegantly for someone else...

Things have been like this from the very start
— others tell me she's just the same with them,
so there's no sense in having it out with her:
she'd laugh and toss her hair, blow a cool smoke-ring
(fluting her tongue the way sophisticates do)
saying: "Sorry about that...", when you know quite well she's not.
Naturally, I've rehearsed a farewell speech
(complete with forlorn settings from de Chirico)
but what's the use? Here she is, talking her beautiful head off,
with half-an-eye for the bloke at the neighbouring table,
shedding opinions like so many hair-pins,
and stubbing her cigarette in the chocolate mousse!

THE WEIGHT OF INSTRUCTION

Beneath a steel-blue sky nearing the end
of Lent, my sister's four-year-old
looks up to me, he needs
his left shoelace tied. Black and white
Nike high-tops like I used to wear,
and I tell him to get his mother to do it.

Outside the window, an oak tree shuffles
its leaves in the wind. Between breezes
I see a nest of sparrows, a mother
pushing her chicks from the high limbs
to try the air's breathless comeuppance
on their own.

It's not how they look
so much as how the mother reminds me
of Sister Ellen from Sunday school classes,
commending us to the church play-yard
after offering no answer for the Trinity —
only psalms and catechisms wrapped
in Latin and incense shrouds.

        The nuns
gave no instructions, just the high-wire
of the commandments, no net below
so you'd better not look down —
the transparent lesson of the soul
simple as a deep breath, learning to fly.

Now I'm rising to find my nephew,
to ask what he learned with the afternoon.
Man to man, we'll each take a shoe and sit
beneath the open kitchen window,
an emptying oak and awkward sparrows,
tying knots until we get it right.

THE REPUBLIC
for David Ignatow

Midnight. For the past three hours
I've raked over Plato's *Republic*
with my students, all of them John
Jay cops, and now some of us
have come to Rooney's to unwind.
Boilermakers. Double shots and triples.
Fitzgerald's still in his undercover
clothes and giveaway white socks, and two
lieutenants—Seluzzi in the sharkskin suit
& D'Ambruzzo in the leather—have just
invited me to catch their fancy (and illegal)
digs somewhere up in Harlem, when
this cop begins to tell his story:

how he and his partner trailed
this pusher for six weeks before
they trapped him in a burnt-out
tenement somewhere down in SoHo,
one coming at him up the stairwell,
the other up the fire escape
and through a busted window. But by
the time they've grabbed him
he's standing over an open window
and he's clean. The partner races down
into the courtyard and begins going
through the garbage until he finds
what it is he's after: a white bag
hanging from a junk mimosa like
the Christmas gift it is, and which now
he plants back on the suspect.
Cross-examined by a lawyer who does his best
to rattle them, he and his partner
stick by their story and the charges stick.

Fitzgerald shrugs. Business as usual.
But the cop goes on. Better to let

the guy go free than under oath
to have to lie like that.
And suddenly you can hear the heavy
suck of air before Seluzzi, who

half an hour before was boasting
about being on the take, staggers
to his feet, outraged at what he's heard,
and insists on taking the bastard
downtown so they can book him.

Which naturally brings to an end
the discussion we've been having,
and soon each of us is heading
for an exit, embarrassed by the awkward
light the cop has thrown on things.
Which makes it clearer now to me why
the State would offer someone like Socrates
a shot of hemlock. And even clearer
why Socrates would want to drink it.

VOCATION

Sunday morning the priest informed all fine young parish men
to consider a vacation,
or at least that's what I thought I heard.

Vowels, misplaced, can alter expectations.
Bitter becomes better,
a lump evolves into a lamp, porcelain, shaped

like a mermaid with one languid hand resting behind her head.
The priest cannot be blamed
for one parishioner's confusion. While I imagined all parish men

boarding the gangway to an ocean liner,
the priest spoke yearningly of friendships made in seminary,
the morning vespers,

Friday dinners of grilled cheese, tomato soup.
Even the oaken bunkbeds, the laundry they did all by themselves.
Until you enter the seminary, the priest said,

nobody can truly understand brotherhood.
Mid-sermon, I remembered what I told a friend last week,
who asked me why a woman — any self-respecting woman —

could remain a Catholic.
Embarrassed, I muttered: Ritual.
Nobody can deny the continuity of a rosary,

Stations of the Cross.
Regular genuflection can prevent arthroscopic surgery,
I might've said, but instead I pretended

the irony was what compelled me,
an anthropologist's native interest in contradictions,
in rites that require me to notice

everything we're usually trained to ignore:
the way somebody's eye twitches during a conversation
about car loans; a neighbor's inability to leave the house

without studying the weather channel's neon forecasts.
At Mass we become inspectors,
running imaginary Geiger counters across our minds,

our bodies,
that unwieldy inner sponge I've come to know as my soul.
If guilt or detection of weakness is a vocation,

then I'm already enlisted,
a lone woman waiting, purse looped over my shoulder,
as I join the single-file line for communion.

SOLSTITIUM SAECULARE

Winter blows on my eaves,
And tall stalks nod in the snow
Pitted by dripping trees.

The strong sun, brought low,
Gives but an evening glare
Through black twigs' to-and-fro

At noon in the cold air.
A rusty windmill grates.
I sit in a Roman chair,

Musing upon Roman fates,
And make my peace with Rome
While the solar fury waits.

I hold my peace at home
And call to my wondering mind
The chaos I came from —

Waste sea and ancient wind
That sailing long I fought,
Unshriven and thin-skinned.

God knows why I perished not,
But made it here by grace
To harbor beyond my thought,

To the stillness of this place.
Here while I live I hold
Young hope in one embrace

With all the ruin of old,
And bless God's will in each;
And bless His word of gold

As far as heart can reach,
Turning the Apostle's page
Or Thomas, who would teach

Peace to the heart's rage.

ALL THIS TALK ABOUT WINNING

Think about it. Rarely are we encouraged,
say, to lose an argument. Why is that?
I mean, in what way shall the first be last,
the last first, if we can't lose an argument?
A precept more genial to the times might run
as follows: Making love is nice only when
each of you desires it. Even this is more
slenderly understood than you would think.

I should have realized how hard it will be to explain
why a camel can't pass through the eye of a needle.
Staying poor is easy if you just remain ignorant of
banking procedures. But that's not entirely my point.

Let's talk first of these photos here, scattered
among the stones. You search, but the one of you is
not among them. What virtue would there be in that anyhow,
what joy, really, in monochrome nostalgia?
You were the one that threw the picnic, after all.
On that April day of sea-change and mixed blessings,
your jugs of dago red and baskets of garlic rolls
fed their clowning: all these stuck-out tongues
and crossed eyes, tipsy Uncle Burt with his fly
half open. When have you and I last earned
such forgetfulness? It is not our faces we should
look for in history. Ask any mother.

Once upon a time
there was a man and a woman
who won and won.
They never cried.
Then one day they lost.
They cried and cried,
heartbeats hurt so.

Back to what I was saying about banks.
What terrible traffic clogging the streets!
In front of Chase Manhattan, taxis squeak and gibber
beneath the weight of profitable afflictions.
Look! So many humans running the marathon this year.
One of them will win. Let us be slow
and note this concourse of strong people.
The rain doesn't stop them, nor the latest
rumors of famine. See how a coin flutters by
the torn blanket there, martyring itself
in the stormdrain.

I'm sick of epistemology.
Some truth is a matter of plain necessity,
obedience to the pulse: a losing of all
argument and a washing of feet, rich for a penny.
It's so hard to grasp — this wholeness in brokenness,
pieces of eggshell in the nest.

BUSH PILOTS

The pilot sprouted from the cockpit,
lobbed backwards till silk puffed,
and his parachute, a tiny mushroom,
held in the wind over fir-crested woods.
Part of our Air Force hobbled out of the sky
toward spears, where it caught,
and tangled wings and splintered fuselage
and cracked its nose cone as silver stars
hit ground in a black and orange noise.

For years we dug up traces of burnt metal,
once thinking our relic was a helmet chip,
rare as the fossil of St. Therese
preserved at our yellow-brick school.
We rummaged in the ruins for bits of wreck,
not pieces of the Dream—that lure of pretty steel.
Like blue angels in a wild blue yonder,
we hitched our saintly wagons to a star,
but fumbled with the junk that fell around us.

October 1: St. Therese

LEONIE, THE PROBLEM
CHILD, EXPLAINS

Therese—our "little Benjamin"—
is the truly odd one, though
I'm sent off to boarding school
for being bad at books and prayer.
Bored by ordinary games,
detesting quadrilles,
she gathers dead birds
under the spiky yuccas, builds
pebbles and shells into little altars.
She'd rather extend her cemetery
than take the sun at Trouville
with Aunt and Uncle Guerin.
But "Hermits" is her favorite game.
She and cousin Marie—
who always gives in
to the little pet—pretend
to have no possessions
but a rude hut and a small cornfield.
Therese demands complete silence,
"contemplation," she calls it,
another big word I can't spell.
There are no quarrels, because
she's the superior. One works,
the other prays. They keep it up
even on the streets, lowering their eyes
and saying the rosary together,
as good hermits should. They imagine
I don't understand. Therese isn't
"obtuse," like me,
or even "intractable,"

but I'm no teacher's pet, no
helpless touch-me-not,
and I have friends at school.
Someday I'll surprise them all:
I'll become a <u>real</u> nun.

October 4: St. Francis

(FEED SQUIRRELS)

feed
squir
rels,

said
ma
ma,

&
the
squir
rels

will
love
you

I
did

&
they
did

now
feed
peo
ple,

said
ma
ma

I
tried

that
too

—

SIGNS OF DEVOTION

Coming down San Pasqual mountain on a day
of high heat, I pass the young Franciscan toiling uphill,
his face sweaty and red as a beet. He is draped
in a brown robe and praying the rosary.

I imagine the coarse robe against his skin,
the heavy cord that binds, Hail Mary's and Our Father's
drying on his lips. I vow to offer him a ride when I return.

Hours later as I travel back up the mountainside
he is still ascending, sandaled feet coated with fine dust.
He tells me he is walking to the Indian mission at Santa Ysabel.
And what he is doing is nothing extraordinary:
only as our mother has asked, just as you
care for your son, live your life, ask your questions.

In an hour or two he reached the clapboard chapel
to pray the stations of the cross. He kneels
before each of the fourteen images:

He passes Jesus condemned to death, bearing the cross —
falling once, then again, and again.
The dark women of Jerusalem weeping.

Children in the late afternoon light say they see Mary
among the blue hillsides and blooming vines.
And I still feel the rough love of that brown robe,
the damp wooden beads.

SONNET FOR FIVE FRANCISCAN SISTERS

when I was twelve, me and Mrs. Bertinetti would
walk the dark of Princeton to Wilson Avenue, she to
St. Francis Church and me to the convent where I
served Mass at 6:30 and with eyes in back of my head
saw Srs. Jean & Damascene, Limbania, Elise & Josephine
starched upright in prayer. The sun's first rays
fired the altar cloths, white as the Angel wings
of the Holy Card tucked like a secret in my Missal.
Somewhere between those mornings when Mass illumined
our faces and I wanted to build tents to hold back
glory from disappearing — it disappeared.
Christ still rises in the Host, but the Missal holds
few secrets and the shine's not there, as for the boy
dazzled, his back to nuns winged with white wimples.

FR. JOE, FRIAR MINOR

Fr. Joe saved breakfast rolls and bread
to feed the birds and small animals
behind the statue of St. Francis.
They asked him to stop because rats
came, but he said, "aren't they life?"
and kept broadcasting crumbs at dawn.

Under the yew tree by the front steps
he used the toe of his sandal to bury
a small dead vole, signing a cross
in the January air. Even the smallest.

The barred window ledges blazed with
African violets—pink, purple, white—
so that browsers stumbling out of the
stacks exclaimed aloud at lush profusion.

If they followed what might be music
to the bindery where Fr. Joe sewed
years into volumes of green buckram
stitching in Mozart, Vivaldi, Bach,
Mahler, Stravinski, he would tell them
about the old German binder who opened
windows to January so his sweat wouldn't
stain the fine materials he worked with.

When you die, what was borrowed
returns to the order.
He returned them unstained.

October 18: St. Luke
(Patron Saint of Painters)

AT THE CHRISTIAN MUSEUM, ESZTERGOM

Scene after holy scene:
George and the dragon, Catherine and the wheel,
Christopher (decommissioned) and his bulk,
Imre, the lily, and the knee bent so,
all, save Sebastian with his loincloth slipped,
wardrobed to the taste of those who brushed.
Even the Crucifixion comes to seem
collage of old motifs in different styles.

How much did they believe?
In Memling's "Man of Sorrows" it's art —
if not quite solely for the sake of art.
Then, with chiaroscuro and receding planes,
technique triumphs.

The man who signed his work MS
blended form and faith.
His Christ, eyes hollow and cheeks gaunt,
has died to pay out all.

Before that, figures on a golden field
portray the mystery suitably estranged.

Piety, said Maritain, cannot replace technique.
Assume the inverse:
faith itself may stem
from forms we have outgrown.

FOR MAX JACOB WHO SAW
CHRIST IN WATERCOLORS

and christ is red rover
he blazes on the wall in watercolors
rachel dances in his brain
and her children trail her heels
in flickering pinks and blues

and the armies of the reich
shake loose from their graves
and they hide and seek
and search and destroy
and the wall is blown down

and christ is reeling in the streets
staining the gutters
with the colors of his blood
and the children are calling
come over come over

GROWING UP WITH GOYA'S SATURNO

In Michoacan he wasn't called Saturno,
nor was he a painting, vulnerable
as the hand that stroked his hair and kept him wild-
eyed as if shocked by his swallowing up of his own
child—perhaps an act he had only fantasized about
but which he had now been forced to commit.

He wasn't confined to the page of an elementary textbook;
he could easily let go the body like a candle
from his grasp and unfold his leg, stepping
down in the dark with a heavy but undetectible
foot. In my world he could blink,
his lashes struck like hatchet marks against his cheeks

as he followed my scent to the bed.
Once there he'd pull back the hair from his ears,
listened for the guilty breathing of a boy
who had not yet coated his tongue with a Credo
or at least three Ave Marias. He did not yet have a name,
but he took up so much space searching

for the smell of my curious fingers, which I had
burdened with my most forbidden openings and which I thought
too heavy to bear the sign of the Cross. I'd stay up
wondering how I'd unstick my limbs from the walls
inside his belly once he'd swallowed me up; how I'd keep myself
apart from that confusion of tides and contractions

from the dirty linens in a room so private, no
guardian angel had yet gone in to explain away the shadows.
He became an anticipation then. He became a Sunday fever,
an excuse from evening Mass. His were the sounds
of beds too passionate to be discreet. His was the light switch
blacked out and made to reappear in some distant house.

He became the collector of the oppressed tongue, that scholar
kept quiet beneath the Eucharist. So when this convocation

claimed its name outside of Michoacan, away from Mexico—
Saturno—it quietly stepped back onto the page, its bones rigid
as print, but with its mouth propped open as if at any moment
it could change its mind— complete what I had once begun.

October 31: All Souls

THE GODS WHO COME AMONG US IN THE GUISE OF STRANGERS
for Charlie Miller

Late nights, with summer moths clinging
to the screens & the shadows of the Old Great
flickering across the tv screen, suddenly,
there would be Charlie's inquisitorial head
peering in the window, the shock of white hair,
followed by the heart-stopping shock
of greeting. Just passing through, he'd say,
and—seeing as the light was on—
thought we might have ourselves a talk.

Did I ever have time enough for Charlie?
Usually not. The story of my life,
of the one, as Chaucer says of someone,
who seems always busier than he is.
Then, abruptly and discourteously,
death put a stop to Charlie's visits.
Summer moths collect still at the windows.
Then leaves & winter ice. Then summer moths
again. Each year, old ghost, I seem
to miss you more and more, your youth spent
with Auden & the Big Ones, words—
theirs, yours—helping you survive
a brutal youth. Too late I see now
how you honored me like those hidden
gods of old who walk among us like
the dispossessed, and who, if you are
among the lucky ones, tap at your window
when you least expect to ask you for a cup
of water and a little of your time.

VOYAGER

Beyond the moon, beyond planet blue
and planet red, each day further
from the sun she floats out toward

the empty dark of X. Having done
what she was sent out years before
to do, she gave up sending even

the faintest signals back to earth,
to bend instead her shattered wings
across her breast for warmth. It is

late, he knows, and knows it will only
go on getting later. He shifts alone
in the late November light before

her grave, as so often he has done
these past five years, to try
and finish what he knows to be

unfinished business and must remain
that way: this one-way dialogue
between the self, and — in her absence —

the mother in himself. Epilogue, perhaps,
to what one man might do to heal
the shaken ghost which must at last admit

just how many years ago she logged off
on her journey. So that now, as darkness
drops about him like some discarded coat,

old but useful, such as his mother used
to wear, he takes it to him, much as
she did, to ward against the cold.

DARK SPACES THOUGHTS
ON ALL SOULS DAY

someone might live
even beyond one self and come
dreaming into the evening of his dream

entering his garden
without a thought in mind
much as a dancer spins with his eyes
focused on a point out there

does not see
stage prop or conductors baton
or the uncurtained
dark eyes of the audience

there are no surprises
yesterday in his garden
there were spring beauties

this is his freedom
the joy of the aged
the solemn moment before
everything goes down

it has to be that day
the stars do fall
and they will fall
so that we may grieve their passing

and perhaps
grow older than any flowering

November 1: All Saints

ST. ISAAC'S CHURCH, PETROGRAD

Bow down my soul in worship very low
And in the holy silences be lost.
Bow down before the marble Man of Woe,
Bow down before the singing angel host.
What jeweled glory fills my spirit's eye,
What golden grandeur moves the depths of me!
The soaring arches lift me up on high,
Taking my breath with their rare symmetry.

Bow down my soul and let the wondrous light
Of beauty bathe thee from her lofty throne.
Bow down before the wonder of man's might.
Bow down in worship, humble and alone.
Bow lowly down before the sacred sight
Of man's Divinity alive in stone.

REUNION

*For Andrew Miller, my dead mother's brother, whose
illness and death last summer gathered our family
around to pay him our respects, my 3 cousins and I
getting together for the first time in a decade, to mourn,
play basketball, and catch up on our lifetimes.*

        The evening cools toward midweek's
promise of relief, a company
of cicadas unconvinced, distracting me
tonight, after 3 days, 20 hours driving,
and these kids downstairs,
keeping the spiders up, their voices choiring,
too hot for dreams born of a little flesh,
too much emergency. He dozes even
as he means to gaze around his sickroom,
seeing (my mother, maybe?)
the family gathered there, easing a man his envy
of other men's success. I wait
a little wind, and watch this aunt, through
several hundred miles set between,
prop his pillowed head, help her husband
to iced water, (too hot for dreams,
too much emergency,) and see, through decades
of married love, a strong man
brought to this, smiling to speak fatigue,
who brought his sons to marveling,
that heart misfiring with all the weight
of 7 decades, unfolding stories
of our family dead, of all bloodlines
imperfectly confected, like a last word
            now on our grandparents'
            hard loving...

                    ✳

        Boys in Fords mock-up *Top Gun,*
blow their own horns cornering,

showing the moon their splendid grins,
like pieces of Time let go,
cruising the neighborhoods downtown
and tracking solace
dragging state routes. Guitars give way
to violins, Ontario's blue sprawl,
blue air and scintillance, blue love raised up
from middle century composing,
more straight on its squared rest,
for all the faults in a made thing, for all
that strictness weighed
deciding not to buy, and all the futures
bought behind the Miracle Motel.
Maybe it's not the time to buy, to step this way
alone and this way into plurals,
into my cousin's mish of Depression facts
and legends, our grandfather's
squandered wealth, and a father after that,
who lost his business at the flashpoint,
as if the words were instruments, were
means to speak a lifetime to himself,
a poem, coincident with horizon trees
and cash crops, with this woman
after all, refined by all the skills of late career,
whatever Park Street says of it, all
of the points glass smooth, the home-run
fields marked and over-run
    with condos.

                *

    I see that ballfield and spiral still,
loose stone, my uncle younger than I am,
       his ripped knee giving under him,

      that tumble and roll brought now
to this sure-footing at his exit, easing the likenesses
      observed in all our gathered faces.

He says he has to think on it. Then
asks me do I pray, feeling the darkness
        taking sides, and if, to pray

        the days be over soon. I pay blood
that respect, and spirit, beneath the jellies
        and wraps of flesh, one of the kids

        here, like riddles worn through,
voice and thrown voice, *sensibly* obscure,
        having bled as family, having lived

        scripts through in old and other centuries,
the subjects left behind, the traumas
        broadcast, gambling on action, the looks

        of blocks, the looks of villages
the interurban visited, before the voice
        had thought or sought the ways
                of speaking it...

                        *

Would he expect them here,
these *voices*, filled by so much light,
who made such tools available
to children, who understood how wood
might take on life for us,
and the conditions of made things,
until we got the minds for it,
preferring our play on the clay courts
the city hosed for winter skaters,
the minds for asterisks of birth,
for early-ending lifetimes?
I take my 2nd glass, after 3 days' temperance,
seeing the hand raised, lacking
strength to hold the call, to bless
demands we made of it,
the scattered children *dying* brought to roost,
walking a yard that would have

spelled successful to his sister, remembering
the voices now, like drumsticks
lightly measuring old drumskins,
and our own words now, talking
the wall-walkers, the shadow-boxers
down, Carl, Brazell, and I,
a 4th picked up to square our ballgame off
at Thornden, imagining our lives
with half a century to boast in, tones
set for whispering, for making points
behind the final currents of a business,
as old as parents *seemed* to be,
feeling our own lives then,
as if there were no ends to them.

Carolyn Alessio teaches creative writing at Southern Illinois University; her work has appeared in ANTIOCH REVIEW, CHICAGO REVIEW, CRAZYHORSE, and QUARTERLY WEST.

Jan Lee Ande's poems have appeared in IOWA WOMAN, YELLOW SILK, and STUDIA MYSTICA. She teaches courses in history of religions, ecopsychology, and writing at The Union Institute College of Undergraduate Studies in San Diego and The Center for Distant Learning.

Sarah Appleton's works include THE PLENITUDE WE CRY FOR and LADDER OF THE WORLD'S JOY, both published by Doubleday. She has been working with the philosophy of Teilhard de Chardin, which is influencing her own work, and has given readings at the Academy of American Poets in New York. She was also a Parks Fellow at Bunting Institute at Radcliffe.

William Baer edits THE FORMALIST. His poems have appeared in POETRY, THE SOUTHERN REVIEW, THE ANTIOCH REVIEW, THE NEW CRITERION, and PLOUGHSHARES. Last year he edited the interviews of Derek Walcott for the University Press of Mississippi.

Kay Barnes lives in Dallas, Texas, and writes for the diocesan newspaper. Her poems have appeared in POETRY, AMERICA, KANSAS QUARTERLY, BAYBURY REVIEW, THE MACGUFFIN, WIND, and other journals and anthologies. She has an M.F.A. in Writing from Vermont College, an M.A. in French from Middlebury College, and an M.A. in English from Marquette University.

Fr. Murray Bodo, author of fourteen books and writer-in-residence at Thomas More College, is a Franciscan priest. His best-selling, FRANCIS, THE JOURNEY AND THE DREAM, has sold over 160,000 copies and has been translated in French, Spanish, Danish, Japanese, Chinese, and most recently, in 1998, Italian. His latest book is TALES OF AN ENDISHODI: FATHER BERNARD HAILE AND THE NAVAJOS, 1900-1961, University of New Mexico Press.

Bruce Bond's poetry appears in such journals as THE PARIS REVIEW, THE YALE REVIEW, THE GEORGIA REVIEW, TRIQUARTERLY, POETRY, and THE NEW REPUBLIC, and his third full-length collection, RADIOGRAPHY (BOA Editions, 1997), recently won the Natalie Ornish Award from the Texas Institute of Letters. Presently he is Director of Creative Writing at the University of North Texas and Poetry Editor for the AMERICAN LITERARY REVIEW.

Sean Brendan-Brown is a graduate of the Iowa Writers Workshop and has published with POETRY IRELAND, BRIAR CLIFF REVIEW, REAL, ROANOKE REVIEW, WEBER STUDIES, WINDSOR REVIEW, THE ANTIGONISH REVIEW, and PRISM INTERNATIONAL.

Ernesto Cardenal, the former Minister of Culture of Nicaragua, has published many books over the years. He lives in a religious settlement, Our Lady of Solentiname, on an island in Lake Nicaragua.

Mike Chasar's poems have recently appeared, or are forthcoming, in THE LITERARY REVIEW, CUMBERLAND POETRY REVIEW, SOUTHERN POETRY REVIEW, NIMROD, SEATTLE REVIEW, SPARROW, and HELLAS.

William Bedford Clark is Professor of English at Texas A & M University. He has published on a variety of topics in American literature and was founding editor of the SOUTH CENTRAL REVIEW. His verse has appeared in CHRISTIANITY AND LITERATURE, ACADEMIC QUESTIONS, XAVIER REVIEW, and SOUTHWESTERN AMERICAN LITERATURE. He is presently at work on an edition of Robert Penn Warren's letters.

Chet Corey is a Covenant Affiliate of the Franciscan Sisters of Perpetual Adoration (La Crosse, Wisconsin). His poetry has appeared in EMMANUEL, SACRED JOURNEY, SISTERS TODAY, AND WINDHOVER, as well as a number of secular publications. He lives in Bloomington, Minnesota, with his wife, Kathy.

David Craig teaches creative writing at the Franciscan University of Steubenville. He has recently published his first novel, THE CHEESE STANDS ALONE, and his sixth collection of poetry, THE ROOF OF HEAVEN. He has a novella, OUR LADY OF THE OUTFIELD, and a collection of essays,

Born in Managua in 1912, **Pablo Antonio Cuadra** is an internationally known poet who considers Nicaraguan Granada his native country. Besides writing, Cuadra also paints, and recently he converted his poems into original tapestries. His works have been widely translated.

Robert Murray Davis teaches at the University of Oklahoma. In two volumes of memoir-social history (MID-LANDS: A FAMILY ALBUM, 1992, and A LOWER-MIDDLE-CLASS EDUCATION, 1996), he writes about a Catholic childhood and college education in the post-

World War II Middle West. He has written and edited eighteen other books and more than a hundred critical and personal essays and poems.

Bruce Dawe is Australia's best-selling poet. His collected edition, SOMETIMES GLADNESS, has sold over 100,000 copies. He is also the winner of numerous literary awards.

Mark Decarteret is a poetry editor for the PORTSMOUTH REVIEW, and his work has appeared in CALIBAN, CHICAGO REVIEW, EXQUISITE CORPSE, LOWELL REVIEW, and SNAKE NATION REVIEW, as well as many other places. His first book, REVIEW—A BOOK OF POEMS, was published last year.

Annie Dillard's PILGRIM AT TINKER CREEK won the Pulitzer Prize for general nonfiction in 1975. She is author of more than ten books, including the memoir AN AMERICAN CHILDHOOD and the novel THE LIVING. The recipient of fellowship grants from the John Guggenheim Foundation and the National Endowment for the Arts, Dillard lives with her family in Connecticut.

Fr. Jeremy Driscoll grew up in Moscow, Idaho, and at the age of twenty-two joined the Benedictine monastery at Mount Angel Abbey in Oregon. He serves as priest and monk there, and teaches graduate theology at the abbey's seminary school. His poems in this anthology come from his book SOME OTHER MORNING (Story Line Press, 1992).

Fr. Gregory Elmer, a monk at St. Andrew's Abbey in Balyermo, California, made profession in 1970, and was ordained in 1976 as a priest monk. Since 1975, he has given Scriptural and contemplative retreats. From 1986-89 he served on the North American Board for East-West dialogue, a group of Benedictine and Cistercian religious, working at mutual encounter, hospitality, and dialogue with Asian monasticism.

David Feela works as an English teacher for Montezuma-Cortez High School and Pueblo Community College. Maverick Press recently published his chapbook, THOUGHT EXPERIMENTS, the 1998 winner of the Southwest Poets Series.

Robert Fitzgerald is generally acknowledged as his generation's pre-eminent translator of classical poetry: THE ODYSSEY (1961), THE ILIAD (1974), and THE AENEID (1983). He was also a gifted poet; his SPRING SHADE: POEMS 1931-1970 appeared in 1971.

Kevin Fitzpatrick is the author of two books of poetry, DOWN ON THE CORNER and RUSH HOUR, both published by Midwest Villages & Voices. He was the editor of the Lake Street Review for many years. He lives in Minneapolis, Minnesota, and works as a civil servant.

Amy Fleury grew up in a small farm town in northeast Kansas. She holds an M.F.A. in Creative Writing from McNeese State University in Lake Charles, Louisiana. Her work has appeared in or is forthcoming from THE LAUREL REVIEW, PRAIRIE SCHOONER, 21ST, and other journals. She is an assistant professor of English at Washburn University of Topeka, where she teaches creative writing.

Linda Nemec Foster's poetry has been widely published in such journals as THE GEORGIA REVIEW, QUARTERLY WEST, MID-AMERICAN REVIEW, INDIANA REVIEW, and NIMROD. Her first full length collection of poems, LIVING IN THE FIRE NEST, was published in 1996 by Ridgeway Press.

Timothy Geiger teaches creative writing at The University of Toledo. His poems have appeared in POETRY, PASSAGES NORTH, and QUARTERLY WEST. He has published five chapbooks, including EINSTEIN AND THE ANTS.

Dana Gioia's poems and translations have appeared in THE NEW YORKER, THE NATION, THE HUDSON REVIEW, and in many other journals. His poetry collections include THE GODS OF WINTER and DAILY HOROSCOPE. He is also the author of CAN POETRY MATTER? ESSAY ON POETRY AND AMERICAN CULTURE. Gioia was a businessman for fifteen years, eventually becoming a Vice President of General Foods. In 1992 he left that to become a full-time writer.

Rigoberto Gonzalez received his M.F.A. from Arizona State University, and his work has appeared in THE JAMES WHITE REVIEW, THE AMERICAS REVIEW, AND MOCKINGBIRD. He was also awarded a University Prize from the Academy of American Poets.

Jerry Harp, when he is not painting, roofing, or moving furniture, is working on a Ph.D. in Literature at the University of Iowa.

Kevin Hart is a Professor of English and Comparative Literature at Monash University in Australia. His work includes NEW AND SELECTED POEMS (Sydney: Harper Collins, 1995) and DARK ANGEL (Dublin: The Daedalus Press, 1996).

David Impastato has published on the subjects of contemporary poetry and Shakespeare on film. He worked for many years as a film director in

Los Angeles, and is currently affiliated with the talking books program at the Library of Congress. In 1997 he edited UPHOLDING MYSTERY, an anthology of contemporary Christian poetry for Oxford University Press. His own poetry has appeared in THE SEWANEE REVIEW and other places.

John Knoepfle is the author of nineteen books and the winner of many grants, including the Rockefeller Foundation, the National Endowment for the Arts, and the Mark Twain Award for Distinguished Contributions to Midwestern Literature. He was awarded an honorary Doctor of Humane Letters from Maryville University in 1996.

Robert Lax, part of that old Merton gang, lives in Greece. The poems we've chosen were drawn from his NEW POEMS (1962).

Denise Levertov has long been a profound spiritual presence in American letters and will be greatly missed. The poems included were gathered from her EVENING TRAIN, which was published in 1992.

Robert Lietz, author of seven collections of poems, is currently teaching at Ohio Northern University. His work has appeared in ANTIOCH REVIEW, CAROLINA QUARTERLY, THE GEORGIA REVIEW, THE MISSOURI REVIEW, THE NORTH AMERICAN REVIEW, POETRY, and PRAIRIE SCHOONER.

Edward Lynskey has, for the past year, worked as a software engineer for Lockheed Martin. (He says he enjoys coding which in format reminds him of the way free verse appears on the page.) Lately he has appeared in COMMONWEAL, AMERICA, CAROLINA QUARTERLY, and PRISM INTERNATIONAL.

Leo Luke Marcello's most recent poetry book is NOTHING GROWS IN ONE PLACE FOREVER (Time Being Books, 1998). His poems have appeared in many journals, such as AMERICA, COMMONWEAL, THE SOUTHERN REVIEW, and IMAGE. He is Professor of English at McNeese State University.

Paul Mariani is Distinguished University Professor at The University of Massachusetts and author of WILLIAM CARLOS WILLIAMS: A NEW WORLD NAKED, and DREAM SONG: A LIFE OF JOHN BERRYMAN. His most recent book of poetry is SALVAGE OPERATIONS: NEW AND SELECTED POEMS.

Paul Marion is the author of nine collections of poetry, including HIT SINGLES and STRONG PLACE. His work has appeared in YAN-

KEE, WISCONSIN REVIEW, BOSTONIA, ALASKA QUARTERLY REVIEW, and elsewhere.

Fr. David May, an erstwhile fan of the Baltimore Colts, is a priest of the Madonna House community, based in Combermere, Ontario, and presently works at the house in North Yorkshire, England. He also served as editor of the community newspaper, RESTORATION, for twelve years.

Janet McCann has had poems in a wide variety of popular and scholarly journals, including CHRISTIAN CENTURY, McCALL'S, SOUTHERN POETRY REVIEW, and AMERICA, as well as in five collections of her own work.

Robert McDowell's first book of poems, QUIET MONEY, appeared from Holt in 1987. His poems, essays, and fiction are published widely. He is the editor of POETRY AFTER MODERNISM and co-translated from Czech Ota Pavel's short stories, HOW I CAME TO KNOW FISH.

Claude McKay's concerns with injustice and with the plight of African Americans led him to a late conversion to Catholicism. His poetry and fiction are widely known. He died in 1948.

Orlando Ricardo Menes is a Floridian of Cuban descent who has just completed a Ph.D. in Creative Writing at the University of Illinois-Chicago. New poems have recently appeared, or will appear, in PLOUGHSHARES, THE ANTIOCH REVIEW, CHELSEA, CALLALOO, and THE AMERICAS REVIEW. He is the author of two collections of poetry.

Fr. Thomas Merton is perhaps the most well-known of all American Catholic poets of the twentieth century. From (mostly) his Abbey at Gethsemani, Kentucky, Merton wrote volumes of poetry, social criticism, and contemplative distillations for New Directions and other presses.

Balazs Mezei is a lecturer in philosophy at the Lorand Eorvos University of Budapest.

Gabriela Mistral, a secular order Franciscan, won the Nobel Prize for Literature in 1945. The poems included here are translated by Doris Dana.

Fred Muratori has been widely published. His collections include DESPITE REPEATED WARNINGS and THE POSSIBLE.

Les Murray: As Auden said a poet should be, Les Murray is local but esteemed elsewhere! His locality is on the East Coast of Australia, at thirty degrees latitude.

Stella Nesanovich is a Professor of English at McNeese State University in Lake Charles, Louisiana. Her poetry has appeared in AMERICA, POET LORE, XAVIER REVIEW, FIRST THINGS, CHRISTIANITY AND LITERATURE, THE CHRISTIAN CENTURY, and elsewhere. She is the author of A BRIGHTNESS THAT MADE MY SOUL TREMBLE: POEMS ON THE LIFE OF HILDEGARD OF BINGEN (Thibodaux, LA: Blue Heron Press, 1996).

Gary Nied teaches English at Cistercian Preparatory School in Irving, Texas, and is a graduate of the Franciscan University of Steubenville. He and his wife Liz have three children and belong to St. Thomas Aquinas parish.

Fr. Robert Pelton is the Director of Priests at Madonna House Apostolate in Canada. He got his Ph.D. from the University of Chicago in History of Religions from the Divinity School. His published books include THE TRICKSTER IN WEST AFRICA, A STUDY OF MYTIIIC IRONY AND SACRED DELIGHT, and CIRCLING THE SUN, MEDITATIONS ON CHRIST IN LITURGY AND TIME.

Arthur Powers worked as a lay missionary in the southern Amazon region of Brazil and subsequently supervised Catholic Relief Service's Brazil program. His poetry has appeared in AMERICA, HIRAM POETRY REVIEW, KANSAS QUARTERLY, SOUTHERN POETRY REVIEW, SOU'WESTER, TEXAS QUARTERLY, and in many other places.

Adélia Prado was born and has lived all her life in Divinopolis, Minas Gerais, Brazil. She earned degrees in philosophy and religious education, and taught religious education in the public schools until 1979. She has been cultural liaison for her native city and has published eight books of poems and poetic prose.

Helen Ruggieri attended St. Bonaventure University among other schools, and has had other poems recently in POET LORE, EARTH'S DAUGHTERS, SYNAESTHESIA, and MAGUFFIN. She teaches in the writing program at the University of Pittsburgh, Bradford, Pennsylvania.

Henry M.W. Russell is an Assistant Professor of English at Franciscan University of Steubenville and the Associate Editor of THE FORMALIST. He is currently at work on a volume on Nathaniel Hawthorne's THE MARBLE FAUN and on THE ENCYCLOPEDIA OF THE CHRISTIAN TRADITION IN AMERICAN LITERATURE.

Richard J. Smith is currently the Program Director at the Spring English Language Center at The University of Ulaanbaatar, Ulaanbaatar, Mongolia, where he served as a Peace Corps Volunteer. Smith, a graduate of the creative writing programs at Michigan and Western Michigan, has published fiction and essays widely, often concentrating in the latter case on the relationship between faith, education and community service.

Ruth Stearns is a graduate of the Franciscan University of Steubenville. She spent a year teaching in Nicaragua and now lives in the New Hope Community in Kentucky.

Kevin Stein has published two books of poems: BRUISED PARADISE and A CIRCUS OF WANT, the second of which won the 1992 Devins Award for Poetry. He has also published chapbooks, essays, and criticism, winning, in the process, the National Endowment for the Arts Poetry Fellowship and three fellowships granted by the Illinois Arts Council.

Frank Stewart has published three books of poems (and seven other books), and for his poetry he has won a Whiting Writers Award. His work, widely anthologized, has been in such journals as PLOUGHSHARES, POETRY INTERNATIONAL, COLORADO REVIEW.

Karol Wojtyla studied literature and drama in Cracow. He worked in a stone quarry and a chemical plant before he began studying for the priesthood in 1942. He was hidden from the German occupation forces by the Archbishop of Cracow and was ordained in 1946. In 1958 he was named bishop of Cracow, and became archbishop in 1964 and a cardinal in 1967. On Oct. 16, 1978, he was elected Pope, the first non-Italian Bishop of Rome in nearly five hundred years.

Amy Yanity received her M.F.A. in Poetry from The University of Pittsburgh; her poems and reviews have appeared in THE PITTSBURGH QUARTERLY, THE BROWNSTONE REVIEW, and THE HARRISBURG REVIEW. She is also a singer and songwriter.

Kathryn Ann Young has published widely, including POET LORE, ZUZU'S PETALS, and SPOON RIVER POETRY REVIEW. She has won many prizes, the Missouri Women's Poetry Award among them, and was on the editorial board for CONFLUENCE in 1997. THE SPINSTER'S MADONNA, a chapbook, was published by Confluence, Indiana in 1996.